WHAT HAPPENS IN SHAKESPEARE

C. B. PURDOM

WHAT HAPPENS IN SHAKESPEARE

A New Interpretation

JOHN BAKER

5 ROYAL OPERA ARCADE, LONDON

Published by
John Baker (Publishers) Ltd.
5 Royal Opera Arcade
Pall Mall, London, S.W.1

Printed in Great Britain by
Clarke, Doble & Brendon, Ltd.,
Cattedown, Plymouth

Perhaps, what I have here not dogmatically but deliberately written, may recall the principles of the drama to a new examination.

Samuel Johnson,
Preface to *Shakespeare* (1765)

CONTENTS

PREFACE

TO add even in a small way to the vast library of books about William Shakespeare and his plays is a serious responsibility. My excuse is that I appear to have something new to say and that as there is no doubt that interest in the plays is intense and shows no sign of diminution I may hope to provide at least some agreeable material for discussion.

What is put forward here is not a version of any earlier theory of Shakespearean interpretation. It was arrived at after I had completed and published my *Swan Shakespeare* in 1932, a work of no particular consequence, but its writing had awakened in my mind an idea that appeared to throw light upon the secret of Shakespeare's art. The following study is the result. It has nothing to do with biographical, textual or historical matters, and is not concerned with philosophical, psychological or any other pre-occupation, but directly with the plays themselves.

The question I ask in these pages and seek to answer is, What is it that Shakespeare does consistently in his plays and more and more perfectly as he advances in command of his art? What, indeed, is the element that makes him the supreme dramatist? Shakespeare's work is so comprehensive, covering the entire scope of drama, that a study of it from this single point of view should be profitable. It has led me to the formulation of what I have ventured to call the fundamental law of drama, to the exposition of which the first part of the book is devoted.

There has been much study of the language of the plays, the images and archetypal myths, the symbols and patterns of meaning, the characters, the stories and their sources, and the themes and their riddles, but too little, perhaps, of their essential quality as drama. Yet it is as drama that Shakespeare is an education in the imagination and the feelings.

I have kept the commentary to the single theme, the dramatic action, thus making the book as concise as possible. I do not suppose that what I have written is other than a first word on a subject to which much more will have to be added. As I have written for the general reader not merely for specialists, I hope the book will help to increase appreciation and enjoyment of the plays as well as have some influence upon their production and playing.

That I owe much to many scholars, commentators and critics there is no need to add except that when I disagree with them and perhaps criticize their opinions adversely I am still conscious of my debt to them and express my thanks.

C. B. PURDOM

PART I

Shakespeare as Dramatist

THE SUPREMACY OF SHAKESPEARE

THAT Shakespeare is the supreme dramatist of the Western world is generally agreed, though not without qualification. No one disputes his supremacy as a poet, but there are those who cavil at his dramatic craftsmanship and find serious defects in his work, and even his whole-hearted admirers do not agree upon what it is in his plays that makes them supreme. From the beginning it was said that while he excelled in the natural vein there were doubts about his art. His early editor, Nicholas Rowe, saw him living under the mere light of Nature, and since then almost every possible fault has been found with him as a playwright, as is shown in the summaries of criticism of the plays contained in the tantalizing two volumes of Augustus Ralli's *A History of Shakespearean Criticism* (1932). The basis of much fault-finding has been that Shakespeare failed to make his plots credible. Fault has also constantly been found on technical grounds such as his neglect of the unities, his careless writing, his mixture of comic and tragic in the same plays, and, if we follow the catalogue of Bradley, *Shakespeare Tragedy* (1904), the short scenes, the soliloquies, the inconsistencies and contradictions, the obscure, inflated and taste-less language, the allegation that Shakespeare speaks rather than the character and so on. Robert Bridges in his impatient lecture *The Influence of the Audience* (1907), argued that Shakespeare was false to his own artistic ideas for the sake of applause, and he found the plays to include bad jokes and obscenities, foolish verbal trifling, brutality and defects of manners, too easy forgiveness of great offences, and inconsistencies or impossible situations, all for the sake of dramatic effect. The limitations of the Elizabethan stage, devoid of scenery, and the fact that his female parts were played by boys, have frequently been regarded as the causes of serious blemishes. Quiller-Couch in *Shakespeare's Workmanship* (1918), which was devoted to considering "just what Shakespeare was trying to do as a playwright", considered it a testimony to Shakespeare's genius that he was able to overcome by poetry the handicaps of his stage as well as he did. Those who have been loudest in praise have often been

13

the most fault-finding, starting with Ben Jonson. A commonplace of some American criticism today is that some of his themes cannot now be accepted, and that greater knowledge and a keener critical faculty are said to cause many of the plays to be entirely out of date.

Indeed, it is possible to wonder why Shakespeare continues to be praised so highly as he is. Everyone is on his knees in obeisance to his poetry, and no one denies his skill in character drawing, but doubts about his ability as a dramatist are never stilled. Mr. T. S. Eliot has said that if he had lived in the seventeenth century "it is quite likely that I should have preferred Beaumont and Fletcher to Shakespeare". He does not stand alone.

Disapproval of Shakespeare in the late seventeenth and eighteenth centuries was due to his lack of conformity with the Italian and French drama then in favour; more recent critics have been influenced by dislike for the stage. There is no doubt that Robert Bridges did not care for the theatre, and I do not recall that Bradley did, while those who find fault with Shakespeare's theatrical ability have, it seems to me, been misled by the consistently low level of popular drama. In his first book of criticism Mr. Eliot said:

> If we had a contemporary Shakespeare and a contemporary Jonson, it would be the Jonson who would arouse the enthusiasm of the intelligentzia.

Perhaps a no more pertinent criticism of the contemporary mind could be made.

I contend that these criticisms are invariably based upon misunderstanding of the nature of drama and indicate failure to recognize what Shakespeare did. While there has been no denying that Shakespeare was a great romantic poet, it still has to be established that he was also the greatest classical dramatist since the Greeks, an aspect of Shakespeare that has never been given the study it deserves. The plays of Corneille and Racine have been accepted as the European classic drama, when the truth is that the plays of Corneille and largely those of Racine are the products of a misconceived dramatic tradition. It has still to be fully recognized that Shakespeare was closer to the classical Greek dramatists and to the dramatic theory of Aristotle than were the revered dramatic poets of France. What an eighteenth-century critic, Edward Young, said of him in relation to the Greeks showed true critical appreciation:

> Shakespeare is not their Son but Brother; their Equal, and that in spite of all his faults.

And the German A. W. Schlegel expressed the truth when in demanding of drama "a deeper, more intrinsic, and more mysterious unity than that with which most critics are satisfied", he went on to say:

> This unity I find in the tragic compositions of Shakespeare, in quite as great perfection as in those of Aeschylus and Sophocles.

What is the quality in the plays of Shakespeare that gives them classic value? The answer is that in these works is contained the essential nature of drama. Thus we are faced with the question, What is drama? a question too seldom asked, or, if asked, answered in a very unsatisfactory way.

THE NATURE OF DRAMA

I propose therefore to devote a few pages to considering the nature of drama, and in doing so I invite brief attention to the classic writer on drama, for although drama has been one of the most highly esteemed forms of literary and artistic activity in all countries, and while dramatic theory has constantly been discussed, there has been no substantial advance upon Aristotle's famous definition made about 330 B.C.

> Tragedy then is an imitation of some action that is important, entire, and of a proper magnitude—by language embellished and rendered pleasurable but by different means in different parts—in the way not of narration but of action—effecting through pity and terror the correction and refinement of such passions.

I quote from the eighteenth century translation of the *Poetics* in Everyman's Library. This famous work consists of a series of lectures or rough notes for lectures—it is not quite certain what it is—and treats of poetry in general; but after saying that all forms of poetry have one thing in common, that they are imitations, and after defining the different forms and discussing what is meant by imitation, Aristotle devotes himself in the fragment that survives to an inquiry into tragedy (apart from a brief dissertation on the epic), thus providing an examination of the nature of drama which has never been surpassed. No apology should be needed for reminding the reader of this discussion, for as a recent critical writer who dislikes the philosopher intensely is bound to admit, the definition I have quoted "is

one of the most extraordinary achievements of the human brain".
More than two thousand years of reflection seems to support that
assertion.

What Aristotle meant by "imitation" has provoked much conflict
of opinion. He pointed out that to imitate is inherent in man, so is
the enjoyment of imitations; but precisely what imitation is, in the
sense in which he was using the word, he did not say, beyond
declaring that the difference between the arts was the means or media
by which they imitate rather than any difference in the things
imitated. According to Plato, who was on the side of the artists,
despite lumping drama, poetry and rhetoric together for exclusion
from his Republic, the thing imitated is that which exists in contemplation, the idea or form in the mind, and it is not impossible
to agree that Aristotle means the same, obscure and often apparently
contradictory as his references are. Thus imitation is not a mere copy
or reproduction of a model but a representation of thought or vision.
That is to say we are not intended to take the imitation for the
original. In short, what is created or re-created by the artist is an
image, or symbol, which stands for the idea of the thing rather than
the thing itself. Were a copy meant, it would necessarily be inferior
to the original; but if the word "imitation" carries the sense of re-
creation, that is to say, if it be understood as poetic creation in the
sphere of imagination, the work becomes of a different nature from
the original, possessing its own standard of perfection. When Aristotle
said that "art imitates nature", he meant that art creates as nature
does, the artist has the creative force that is in nature.

If there is difficulty about the meaning of "imitation" there should
be less over the word "action", for Aristotle is much clearer in his
use of the latter word, though we have always to remember that what
we have is an imperfect report of what he said rather than his own
written text. By "action" he means "a thing done", and in the course
of the work he uses "action", "doing", and "drama" as more or less
equivalent terms. Action in Aristotle's sense is not action in general
but "an action", a particular action, an experience. Furthermore, it
is not what has actually happened, but the kind of thing that might
happen according to probability or necessity. Drama, that is to say,
is not history, it is poetic invention. All this is explicit.

As a matter of history, "the thing done", the performance, was
originally song and dance; later it was specifically what the poet did
as actor in conjunction with the chorus; later still it was what three

actors did with the chorus, the first or leading actor maintaining his place.

The dramatic action, according to Aristotle, has to be "important", that is to say not commonplace or everyday; "entire", that is to say, having a beginning, a middle, and an end, making a whole or complete action; of a proper "magnitude", that is to say, it must be of a length according to the nature of the action, and the more extensive, "the more beautiful will it be", though magnitude is not "regulated by the hour-glass"; the "language" being pleasurable "by different means in different parts", which means not the actors' parts but the parts of the work; in the way "not of narration", that is to say not by a description of what is done but the doing of it by the actors; the whole effecting through "pity and terror", the correction and refinement, that is to say the purgation, of the soul.

There is dispute as to whether Aristotle meant that the object of tragedy through the dramatic action was to excite pity or fear, and though there is further dispute about what is meant by the purgation or purification, the *katharsis*, there is no doubt that these are the most important elements. The question is: Is the action of the drama intended to excite or reproduce in the spectator the emotions represented as experienced by the characters, so that he too may experience them and thus be purged in his own soul, or is the action intended to present those emotions purified in image or symbol, so that the spectator may enter into them imaginatively without reproducing them? I think there is no doubt that the spectator is intended to experience them imaginatively. That is, the purification takes place through participation in the dramatic action: the purgation or release from the emotions, not in experiencing the emotions themselves. That is not the same as Tolstoy's doctrine that the aim is to communicate emotions, for what has to be communicated, in drama, is purgation through the symbol, the liberation contained in the conclusion or object of the work. The purgation is effected through the completion of the dramatic action: in the redemptive suffering inherent in tragedy the natural impulses are purged. The purging is from egotism, the egocentricity that is the destructive element in the soul, and is contained in the resolution or reconciliation that is the end of the action. We should understand that what happens is the purification of the soul from the pain and pleasures of the egoistic self, what Plato meant in the *Timaeus* by being "born again in beauty inwardly".

Aristotle proceeded to define the six parts of a tragedy as the fable, or plot; manner, or the characters; diction, or the language; sentiments, or the thought or idea; decoration, or the setting or spectacle; and music, or song. The most important of these six parts, "the soul of tragedy", he said, is "the combination of incidents or the fable", because the fable carries and completes the action.

What he may have said about comedy apart from a few remarks is lost, but the definition may be considered to apply also to that category of drama, remembering that comedy is concerned with comic action, and that the purgation is through laughter: through its licence and free speech the soul is set free.

Of the importance of the first character Aristotle says little, apparently taking it for granted. He does say, however, that unity of plot does not depend merely upon having one man as hero, by which I think he means that unity is in the action, for while many things may happen to one man and while many other men may be involved, drama is concerned with a single action. All the examples of the classical Greek drama we possess are concerned with the situation of a single person, man or woman, whose "action" constitutes the drama, the other persons existing in their relation to him or her in that action. This first character, or protagonist, is usually named in the title of the play as Oedipus, Electra, Antigone, Orestes, Medea, and Hippolytus, though sometimes, as in *Agamemnon*, the protagonist is another person, Clytemnestra.

As the performance of a Greek play was a religious ritual, "drama" being related to "rite", its action could not be something actual: of necessity it was mythical, a vision concerned with the soul. A drama contained a protagonist in a perilous situation, the working out of the situation being the action, its completion leaving the character defeated, yet purified, inwardly restored to his real "self". Aristophanic comedy placed a central character in a comic predicament which was resolved in laughter. The point of the plot as of the action was completion. In a recent study of the *Poetics*, Professor Else makes the important suggestion that *katharsis* was that completion, for he interprets it as "the carrying to completion through a course of events involving pity and fear, the purification of those painful or fatal acts which have that quality". That is to say the value of the work of drama was contained in its conclusion.

As it is no part of my purpose to discuss the questions raised by Greek drama I will mention briefly that there was a rapid decline in the fourth century B.C., for the comic elements, always a part of the dramatic festivals, became predominant, while naturalism and spectacle increased until they wholly occupied the stage. Practically nothing remains of these plays, but it is clear that the decadence of the drama, that is to say the disappearance of "action" in the Aristotelian sense, under the influence of the demand for naturalistic entertainment became complete. There followed Roman drama, which was largely spectacle, its poetic and dramatic qualities being small. The plays of Seneca that were to count for so much centuries later were not written for performance, for the theatre was by then beneath contempt. With the decay of the Empire the drama went out entirely, and the Church excommunicated all who had to do with the stage.

After the slow revival of drama in the Middle Ages, in connection with dramatizations of Biblical stories and the lives of the saints, the writing of morality plays for religious instruction, and finally a story-telling secular drama, the Italians of the fifteenth century discovered what they considered to be the three dramatic unities of time, place and action in re-discovering Aristotle. But this error had far-reaching effects, for the unity Aristotle insisted upon was that of dramatic action, that a drama should be complete, a whole, not a narration of a number of incidents but an action that for the protagonist was one; he said nothing about time or place.

The "unities", however, were made more or less the basis of Italian and afterwards Spanish drama, and were adopted by the French in the early seventeenth century. They had already been transplanted to England, fortunately without flourishing, though Ben Jonson had a mind for them. Shakespeare did not observe them, having a better and more truly Greek idea. They had their effect, however, upon English drama through French examples, and John Dryden did much to recall them, but the English point of view was expressed by Sir Robert Howard, answering Dryden in 1668:

> I shall not discommend any Poet that dresses his Play in such a fashion as his Fancy best approves.

This rebellion against form, which was supposed to be consistent with the "natural" drama of Shakespeare, that drama can be anything the playwright pleases so long as it can be made to exist upon the stage, has remained the rule for playwrights ever since, with disastrous results, for the absence of true form in drama, which was never more evident than today, has led writers much astray.

Apart from discussion of the "unities" no addition was made to dramatic theory until early in the nineteenth century when Samuel Taylor Coleridge (1808) in his philosophical critical exposition declared that the drama "is not *a copy* of nature; but it is an imitation . . . the language inspired by the passion, the language and passion modified and differenced by the character". His contemporary, the formidable Georg Wilhelm Friedrich Hegel formulated in his *Aesthetik* (1818) a theory of drama as "conflict", in which the hero's personal life was given a form of dramatic activity; this made a substantial contribution to the subject and had great influence upon German romantic drama. Friedrich Nietzsche's *The Birth of Tragedy* (1872) contained the poetic and profound idea of tragedy as a "vision" arising out of the satiric dance, in which the spectators transform themselves and become one with the dancers, which idea had no influence at all. It was the French critic Ferdinand Brunetière who, in 1894, produced the idea of drama as the "conflict of will", which prepared the way for twentieth-century drama; for he was followed by the Irish Bernard Shaw with his idea of drama as "discussion" (1898), which he discovered in Henrick Ibsen, by the Scottish William Archer with his idea of drama as "crisis" (1912), forming a trinity of ideas that hold their own in drama today.

I am aware that in this cursory summary I have given no consideration to the theories of theatrical representation, which led to much experimentation, which is perhaps coming to its head today, though none of the theatrical theories of the part has held its own, and all may be regarded as epiphenomenal. Throughout, the practical tendency of the stage was towards naturalism, which contains no theory of drama; for to be natural is the constant disposition of those who look for a way of working other than to observe the discipline of art. I have, too, left out of account the Elizabethan contribution, to which I now come, and in particular to the contribution of Shakespeare.

THE ELIZABETHAN CONTRIBUTION

Before Shakespeare came to London the Elizabethan drama was already established, for the first public theatre had been built in 1576 when Shakespeare was at school at Stratford-on-Avon. Then the drama had the means of providing a popular entertainment, too popular for the liking of the puritanical tradesmen of London City. There can be no doubt that there was reason for offence at the gaudy playhouses and their conscienceless playwrights, as Sir Philip Sidney admitted in his magnificent *Apologie for Poetrie* in 1581, saying that current English tragedies and comedies "observed rules nyther of honest civilitie, nor of skilful Poetrie", being "faulty both in place and time, the necessary companions of all corporall actions". This was Sidney's attempt to get his countrymen to recognize at least some dramatic discipline by observing that of the Italian dramatic theories; but though he had much influence the energy in dramatic writing that possessed the Elizabethan age was not deflected by it, for the dramatists most fortunately paid more heed to Sidney's poetic doctrine, when he declared of playwrights:

> And doe they not knowe, that a Tragedie is tied to the lawes of Poesie, and not of Historie? not bound to follow the storie, but having libertie either to faine a quite newe matter, or to frame the history to the most tragicall convenience.

Adding words to which too much emphasis cannot be given:

> Againe, many things may be told, which cannot be shewed, if they knowe the difference betwixt reporting and representing.

Sidney was, however, much perplexed by "this play matter", for he was himself an unsuccessful dramatist.

Some years later with the advent of the young Christopher Marlowe a new structural principle was introduced into drama, Greek rather than Roman, for Marlowe broke the influence of Senecan tragedy that was all the rage, and in *Tamberlaine the Great* (1587-8), wrote the first wholly original English dramatic work. It was an enormous achievement, for in Marlowe's play, English drama, derived from the tradition of popular medieval drama to which the young men from the universities were giving a Roman touch, became entirely different in form and spirit from all that had preceded it. In *Tamberlaine* the narrative play was elevated not merely by sublime verse but by a new conception of drama into an art of a supreme order, and the conception of a protagonist from whose point of view the action was unfolded became the structural form. Marlowe's achievement thus laid the foundation of English drama, and that Shakespeare derived his fundamental notion of drama from him there can be little doubt. The two men were of the same age, but Marlowe was productive much earlier, and his brief career was practically over as Shakespeare's began. *Tamberlaine* is by no means a perfect drama, but in grandeur of language, poetical energy, and positive dramatic insight displayed in the conception of dramatic action contained in it, the play remains a work of the highest value.

William Shakespeare, the greatest product of the first Elizabethan age, is a mystery. That he came from Stratford-on-Avon we know, and the first reference to his presence in London is in 1592, when he was twenty-eight. His last play was performed in 1613 and his death took place in 1616, so that in a period of approximately twenty-two years, or a little more, he wrote thirty-seven plays, two long poems, a collection of sonnets, and some other small pieces. That Shakespeare must have had deep experience before he became a playwright as well as afterwards there can be no doubt, for his works could not have been the product of idle dreaming; but of the facts of his life we know next to nothing.

Which was Shakespeare's first play is uncertain. The best authority has it that the three *Henry VI* histories (1591–2) were the first, but he may have written *Titus Andronicus* earlier, possibly *Richard III*, or even *The Comedy of Errors*, which would mean that he was in London earlier than is supposed. There are arguments to support all these contentions. Yet it is tempting to think that he was provoked to imitate Marlowe, as well as to prove that he could excel the other university playwrights, and it is certain that Shakespeare wrote as he did because he had the same perception of the nature of drama as had the Greeks, though it cannot be denied that he belongs to the tradition of English popular drama. He had greater genius than Marlowe, but adopted from him the principle of a central character whose presentation of his situation constitutes the dramatic action, the play being intended for the participation of a popular audience appreciative of great ideas and splendid speech.

What Shakespeare thought about the nature of drama he made Hamlet say in his discourse to the players:

> ... the purpose of Playing, whose end, both at the first and now, was and is to hold as 'twer the Mirrour up to Nature, to shew Vertue her owne Feature, Scorne her owne Image, and the verie Age and Bodie of the Time, his forme and pressure.   (3.2)

He was addressing the players, but these words go far beyond what actors have to do, and indicate Shakespeare's mind after ten years' experience of playwriting. The famous words cannot be too much studied from this point of view. What the actor has to do on the stage, the dramatist has to do in writing for the actor: to hold up what is seen as in a mirror for the actor to hold up in his playing to the audience: the play is not the mirror but what is reflected in it, and what is reflected is not, as it were a "slice of life", but one's own mind reflecting the impersonal self and Nature in imagination. A play is Nature, says Shakespeare, not as she is, but as she appears in reflection, that is to say, it is more than can be seen directly with the eyes, being an image, or re-creation. Shakespeare's "Nature" comprises "Vertue" and "Scorne", also the "Age and Bodie of the Time", which is the experience of life, in which there is "forme", the eternal Nature, and "pressure", the appearance in experience.

It is worth noting, perhaps, that the words quoted do not appear in the First Quarto, and in the absurd *Fratricide Punished* they read "in a mirror one may see his own failings", which indicates how little comprehension the actors had of the sense of the play. Yet in these remarkable words it is made clear that Shakespeare knew what he was doing. He was a master because he possessed the secret of the dramatic art. What is offered in the play is an imaginative sharing or participation in a vision or image of the experience, not the experience itself, and certainly not identification with the character. I do not say that Hamlet's words are a complete statement of the nature of drama, for the words were addressed to the actors. The dramatist, himself, has more to do, as the plays show, but what he has to do can, I think, be better understood if these key words be kept in mind.

I shall come to this in a moment, but in the meantime I wish to observe that contrary to Shakespeare, as he always was, Ben Jonson none the less recognized the same principle of drama as Marlowe and Shakespeare, but was unfortunately misled by the "unities", which he thought a superior idea. In the prologue to *Volpone* (1605) he declared of himself:

> The laws of time, place, persons he observeth
> From no needful rule he swerveth.

It was such statements, as well as what he wrote in *Discoveries* (1630), that gained Jonson the name of classic dramatist. But writing as he thought in the classic manner he had insufficient respect for what is essential, which explains why his plays have an archaic structure, and in particular why his ambitious tragedy *Sejanus* is a failure. Jonson's influence, I am inclined to say, had more than a little to do with the inability to understand what Marlowe and Shakespeare had done, which led to the decline of the drama in England throughout the Carolian age to the closing of the theatres.

Without going into all this, I now invite the reader to consider a description of the nature of drama as it is found in Shakespeare, which seems to be a true definition of the Shakespeare play, that it is *a work performed by actors in words and movements, containing the story in action of a problem confronting a protagonist, leading to a crisis in which the problem is resolved, the action being presented from the point of view of the protagonist after the crisis.*

I regret that I cannot make this definition shorter. It contains what I venture to call "the fundamental law of drama", which is not a "law" invented by myself, but inherent in Shakespeare's plays, as I shall attempt to show, and derived from them. By "law" I mean a practical discipline based upon a clearly defined concept. It is the informing principle of the work in which is contained the completed form, inherent not imposed: in short, it is the dramatic action. In other words, what I call the "law" is the description of the dramatic action to which the play owes its form and organic content. And while in these pages I shall be concerned to follow the recognition and development of this "law" in Shakespeare's plays, I suggest that it is the essential element in drama as a form of art for it incorporates and carries further the Aristotelian definition. Without its observance drama does not exist, only theatrical entertainments. There are rules of a technical order in playwriting, which are not to be confused with the law of drama, but with these I do not deal.

Here I confine attention to the "law" as it appears in Shakespeare's work, and my particular point is that his recognition of this "law" is what makes his plays the great dramatic works we know. At the same time, I do not want it to be thought that in concentrating attention upon this one element I ignore the fact that drama has different aspects at different times, neither am I trying to suggest that the themes, characters and scope of drama are in any way limited. I am concerned with the essential element that continues unchanging, the element that belongs to the nature of drama and causes it to possess organic form and content, so that, whatever the changes, in principle it remains the same.

THE FUNDAMENTAL LAW OF DRAMA

I ask the reader to consider this "law" in more detail.

(1) A *play is a work performed by actors in words and move-ments.* . . . A written work is no more than a portion of a play, for actors are required to present the characters, speak the words, and perform the action. This may seem to contradict Aristotle, who, in arguing that tragedy is superior to epic poetry, declared that tragedy, too, "reveals its power by mere reading", but he was striving to point out the unity of the forms of art. Certainly a tragedy can be enjoyed in the reading, but reading is an altogether different act from parti-cipating as a spectator in a performance, as everyone's experience confirms. It is the presence of the audience that constitutes the per-formance and calls the play into being, for an audience is not, in Locke's words, a group of "lazy lookers-on" but participants. The drama becomes theirs, and the arts of dramatist and actor are intended to bring the audience into the action of the play so that they may live through and complete the dramatic experience. The mistakes, suffering, and death of the hero are for them, the predicaments and absurdity of the comedian are theirs too.

In this connection I draw attention to what Bernard Shaw said when putting forward his idea of drama as discussion in a chapter added to his *The Quintessence of Ibsenism* in 1913, after he had had considerable experience as a dramatist. Saying that the technical novelty of the Ibsen and post-Ibsen plays was the introduction of the discussion until it "interpenetrates the action", he went on to add that it was also . . .

> as a consequence of making the spectators themselves the persons of the drama, and the incidents of their own lives its incidents, the disuse of the old stage tricks by which audiences had to be induced to take an interest in unreal people and improbable circumstances, and the sub-stitution of a forensic technique of recrimination, disillusion, and penetration through ideals to the truth, with a free use of all the rhetorical and lyrical arts of the orator, the preacher, the pleader, and the rhapsodist.

This is a penetrating account of what happens when in the perform-ance the spectators see aspects of themselves in the characters, and is at least the beginning of the participation to which the play invites them. The spectator sees himself in the play as he would like to be, or fears to be, in situations that have relation to his own life. That is what gives reality to the play. In that sense he takes the play into himself, and to convince the spectator of such reality is the playwright's and actor's task. But it is necessary to take the matter further than Bernard Shaw was prepared to go. What the dramatist asks from the audience is not identification with the characters but participation in the action. To go to plays to identify ourselves with the characters and to get satisfaction out of the sublimation to which such identification may lead, is not, I suggest, the particular dramatic experience. To see ourselves in a character is not enough, and merely to identify oneself may be to misuse the experience, for we are not involved with the characters as real people, and the attempt to secure this involvement destroys the drama. The spectator is not Brutus, or Hamlet, or Lear but surrenders himself to a spell, to the communication of a vision in which unconscious forces are made to operate in his mind. What we are required to do is to share in an experience not our own, and by sympathetic imaginative reception to be transformed through it. We are required to be more than mere identifiers, as we are more than lookers-on : we have to enter into, to accept, to take in from the dramatist the vision he offers in the play. In short, the dramatic experience is not simply emotional, as if we shared in suffering that seemed rather like our own, neither is it a mere reaction : it is also an exercise of the mind. Drama is not simply a conventional form of writing, but a special way of expressing the results of thought. What is done in drama is not possible in any other way. In the acted play man speaks to man, and an experience is shared in the presence of others. The essential element is the shared experience in the vision, made possible by the offering of the actors in the presence of the audience.

(2) . . . *containing the story in action of a problem confronting a protagonist.* . . . A play is a story, an invention, not a record of actual events, but the transformation of Nature into the imaginatively conceivable. Furthermore, as a story it differs from a novel in not being simple narrative and not needing a story-teller. The story exists as an action. Moreover the action is visual : it is "a moving body of imagery". Sight and hearing, and the senses as well as the mind are engaged, for the play addresses the complete man. Further, the action is of a particular kind, it concerns a problem (or predicament or difficulty) confronting a protagonist—the play's first or leading character. Note that it is not any kind of problem, or a number of

problems, but the protagonist's problem. It is essentially a personal problem, the problem of a man's inner being, the action of the play being the setting in which he encounters himself. In the mirror we see the idea or image, the characters and situations not as they actually exist, though they seem to be, but as they are reflected in the mind of the protagonist who holds *his* mirror up—in the play—for the audience to look into. The seeming is the only element of illusion: we see the actors, who are not the actual persons, but *seem* to be, neither are they presented as those persons but as they *seem* to be in the vision.

Note, especially, the Greek word "protagonist", the constituent part of which means "first". This, I suggest, is the essence of the thing. There can be only one first character. To attempt to recognize more than one is to misunderstand the very nature of drama, and a playwright setting out to introduce more than one protagonist does not write a play because dramatic structure will not allow it. The reason for this is that a play is a particular kind of concentrated writing, the unity of which depends upon the single character. And the important matter is how the problem confronting the character is formulated, for until it is rightly formulated it cannot be resolved. Thus it is essential to know what the problem is, for a problem not rightly stated continues in its imperfection, or changes into another problem.

(3) ... *leading to a crisis in which the problem is resolved.* ... The crisis or climax is that to which the action leads and for the sake of which the play has been written. Unity in drama is present in the completion of the action. The spectator must be convinced at the opening that the action will be completed, though there should be nothing obvious or mechanical in the process. The crisis is the most important moment of the play, for in it the problem is resolved, or, to use a favourite word, the "pattern" is completed. What happens in tragedy is the defeat of the hero, and in defeat his re-generation, for it is of the nature of tragedy that the protagonist's destruction leads to his salvation, which is why tragedy is tolerable, even exhilarating. In comedy, the climax is the culmination of the protagonist's predicament, how some foolishness of behaviour, weakness of character or other obstacle that interferes with happiness is overcome. In farce, the climax is the solution of the complexities of an absurd and artificial situation into which the protagonist has got himself placed.

From the idea of the redemption of the hero in tragedy or the resolution of the comic problem in comedy emerges the feature of Greek drama, the new birth. Thus the drama, through the reconciliation it establishes, is fulfilment in a new life: Dionysus torn to pieces but restored is the myth to which the drama is dedicated.

This idea of a problem to be resolved applies to art in all its forms and is not peculiar to drama; what belongs to drama is the manner of its presentation.

To say that drama contains a personal problem that is resolved is not the same as to say that it does not contain mystery. Every work of art contains to a greater or less extent more than can be explained. What I am considering here is not the dramatic mystery but the principle of working. Merely to state a personal problem and to bring it to a solution would not make drama. There must be in the solution that which raises the action to its greatest height, for something has been achieved.

(4) . . . *the action being presented from the point of view of the protagonist after the crisis.* As a play is not a mere narration of events but action brought to a conclusion so the action leading to it is from the hero's point of view. What makes drama is the re-creation of events, the communication of a vision, in which the protagonist—or hero, or leading character—views the persons involved, including himself, from the point reached when the tension is released and the conclusion reached. This idea of "vision" is not to be confused with the "flash back" device used in some plays and often adopted in films, which is no more than a method of naturalistic story telling. It is not a going back into history, repeating what then took place, relating the events as they could have been seen by an onlooker, but the re-experiencing of the events not as the past or as the present but in the timelessness of consummation. In this timeless view the hero is delivered from the ego-centricity of time, he escapes from the prison of his ego. Thus it is of the very essence of the dramatic hero that his ego has been transformed in the course of the action.

A Shakespeare play is therefore a reflection or meditation upon experience. It is concerned not with what is actual but with the conceivable, and within those limits we are brought, in comedy, into the realm of fulfilled desire, in tragedy, to relief from frustrations and the effects of disaster, and the world of the play is wholly within the vision of the protagonist. This is the central feature of the argument contained in this book, that the plays contain vision in which the self-being of the leading character attains truth, that they are concerned with images of human existence, not descriptions of real people or accounts of actual events but contemplation upon them.

The virtue of my argument is that if it be the manner of its making, as St. Thomas Aquinas said, that decides the nature of a work—its structure, the integrity of its form, the truth of its purpose, and the validity of its aim—the study of Shakespeare's plays from this point of view, or at least with this question in mind, cannot fail to be rewarding.

WHAT CRITICS HAVE SAID

Although I have not discovered any commentator upon Shakespeare or theorist upon the drama who has considered the nature of Shakespearean drama in the sense in which I have defined it, there are indications of approaches to it. One has the impression of scholars drawing near to the solution of problems of interpretation only to draw back at the critical moment, when, had they pressed on, they might have reached the climax of their efforts. I ask the reader's attention to some evidence for this in the writings of a few eminent critics, without attempting anything approaching a full survey.

A. C. Bradley is the Shakespeare critic who still overshadows all others in this century. Few critics in this country or America escape from his influence, and most of those who attempt to do so appear to remain in awe of his authority. In the first chapter of *Shakespearean Tragedy* (1904), Bradley answers the question, What makes a Shakespearean tragedy? by saying:

> . . . it is pre-eminently the story of one person, the hero, or at most of two, the "hero" and the "heroine" . . . we may . . . speak of the tragic story as being concerned primarily with one person.

He had the idea of a leading character, "or at most of two", the tragedy consisting of that character's suffering and death, and he made the statement that Shakespeare "presents the catastrophe as a thing foreseen . . ." by which he meant that it was necessary. I, too, mean that it was "foreseen", though in a sense different from Bradley's. He goes on to say that although there may be a conflict between two persons, or groups, or parties:

> . . . yet that which engrosses our interest and dwells in our memory at least as much as the conflict between them is the conflict within one of them . . . a conflict of forces within the hero's soul.

This shows that Bradley had the idea of drama and had he developed it he would have written a different book; but his real interest was in character: "action", he said, "is essentially the expression of character". It is now coming to be suspected that Bradley has led several generations of commentators astray through this excessive interest in character; for what he declared to be his intention at the opening of his book, he very quickly departed from. To be candid, story-telling was what Bradley looked for, which led him to find much extraneous matter in the plays "neither required by the plot nor essential to the development of character". The soliloquies, in which the protagonist takes the audience into his confidence, he found particularly objectionable:

> It will be agreed that in listening to a soliloquy we ought never to feel that we are being addressed.

This is the reverse of the truth, and shows how far Bradlay got away from his own too tentative idea of drama, for the soliloquy exists to enable the audience to be fully conscious of being addressed. He found "gnomic passages", which he could not stand, for he was looking for nature, not imagination. I shall return to Bradley when the plays are being considered.

Dr. J. Dover Wilson says in his excellent little The Essential Shakespeare (1932):

> Shakespeare asks every spectator, every reader, to sympathise with his hero, to feel with him, to place himself in his shoes, to understand his situation, and to attempt, in imagination, a solution.

That indeed is true, but how this sympathy is evoked is important, and what the dramatist does to evoke it in the structure of his play Dr. Wilson does not consider, neither does he deal with it in his great editorial work on the particular plays; but here there is a close approach to what I am saying without the explicit statement of it.

Mr. T. S. Eliot goes so far as to declare in his essay on "Rhetoric and Poetic Drama" (1919):

> The really fine rhetoric of Shakespeare occurs in situations where a character in the play sees himself in a dramatic light.

Were Mr. Eliot to have considered what "a dramatic light" meant he might have reached what I am trying to say, for the "dramatic light" is that in which the protagonist sees himself and all other characters in the play. It is precisely that. Yet Mr. Eliot's interest appears to be in words, in rhetoric, for he also writes:

> A speech in a play should never appear to be intended to move us as it might conceivably move other characters in the play, for it is essential that we should preserve our position as spectators, and observe always from the outside though with complete understanding. . . . when a character *in* a play makes a direct appeal to us, we are either the victims of our own sentiment, or we are in the presence of a vicious rhetoric.

This suggests that Mr. Eliot approaches the play as narrative and expects story-telling. But story-telling is subordinate to the essential object of drama, which is to move the spectator and to secure his participation, which it does through dramatic action, not in the manner of story-telling. In dramatic action, the spectators are participants, not lookers-on, and what is said with the object of moving the other characters is intended much more to move them. The direct appeal of the protagonist, so far from being vicious rhetoric, is the stuff of drama, for the object is to transport the spectator into imaginative participation in the protagonist's vision. However, in his essay "Shakespeare and the Stoicism of Seneca" (1927), Mr. Eliot has this significant remark.

> . . . there is, in some of the great tragedies of Shakespeare, a new attitude. It is not the attitude of Seneca, but is derived from Seneca. . . . It is the attitude of self-dramatization assumed by some of Shakespeare's heroes at moments of tragic intensity. It is not peculiar to Shakespeare; it is conspicuous in Chapman: Bussy, Clermont and Biron, all die in this way. Marston . . . uses it; and Marston and Chapman were particularly Senecan. But Shakespeare, of course, does it very much better than any of the others, and makes it somehow more integral with the human nature of his characters. It is less verbal, more real.

Yes, indeed, the hero, or protagonist, self dramatizes, but he does more: he "dramatizes" the other characters also. One gets the impression from this passage as from other remarks by Mr. Eliot that he is reluctant to approach Shakespeare except in the company of lesser dramatists. Can it really be maintained that the tragic intensity of Chapman's or Marston's or any other Elizabethan's heroes is on the same level as Shakespeare's? Is it not true that Shakespeare's are not merely more human and more real, but that they do more efficiently and with purer imaginative power what a tragic hero should do?

Shakespeare's dramatic art is greater, indeed on a different level, from that of his contemporaries because he had a clearer conception of the function of the tragic hero. The entire drama is that of the hero, for it is his release from subjection to himself and to outer circumstances that makes the drama. The drama is, in short, concerned with a new kind of consciousness, which is most conspicuously evident in Shakespeare. Mr. Eliot, in common with most critics, finds the poet's function to be "not intellectual but emotional", but he has shown in his own work that while the poet works instinctively, as the bee makes honey, yet he also works with the divine intellect, and that the consciousness awakened by drama is intellectual-emotional, not exclusively the one or the other.

That Harley Granville Barker did not probe more deeply into the nature of drama is a matter of regret, for he was himself a playwright of delicate and keen perception as well as one of the most important stage producers and critics of Shakespeare. Although in his famous *Prefaces to Shakespeare* (1923–48) he had much of the highest value to say about the plays from a stage-craft point of view, the more one studies the *Prefaces* the more one gets the impression that Barker exercised his subtle mind too much upon questions of character, time and place, being greatly under Bradley's influence. Thus he was very ready when he met with a problem that appeared to be insoluble to come to the conclusion that Shakespeare was clumsy, or lacked craftsmanship. These are dangerous conclusions. In the light of the fundamental law I fear that much of Barker will have to be re-written, though I have the impression as I read him that he hovered on the brink of recognizing it; for in a lecture delivered in 1923, *From Henry V to Hamlet*, Barker did, it seems to me, put his finger on the essential element that the drama is what is contained in the mind of the protagonist. Discussing *King Lear* he says:

> And for the storm itself, he shows it us in its full play as a reflection of that greater storm that rages in the mind of Lear. . . . For that storm, as Shakespeare knows now is the really dramatic thing, moreover it is the only thing that his art can directly and satisfactorily present.

The "really dramatic thing" was what Barker was in search of, but he did not realize the significance of what he had said, and when he came to write his preface upon *Lear* he seems to have forgotten it. He approached the idea again in his discussion upon *Hamlet* when he said:

. . . there is literally nothing in the play which is not, in some way or another, germane to its story or illustrative of Hamlet's character, or a consequence, direct or indirect, of what he does or leaves undone.

I should put it that there is nothing in the play not germane to the situation in which the hero was placed, or that does not arise out of it. For it is not with what Hamlet was at any other moment that we are concerned but with him at the particular moment of the drama: that moment contains the dramatic action and is complete in itself. Although in natural time it occupied days and months, natural time is banished from drama. In the introduction to his first volume of his Shakespeare series Barker wrote:

> All great drama tends to concentrate upon character; and, even so, not upon picturing men as they show themselves to the world like figures on a stage—though that is how it must ostensibly show them— but on the inner man.

The truth underlying what I have called the fundamental law is that drama concentrates upon the "inner" man, not upon personal idiosyncrasies, or the things that separate him from others, but upon the inner man's relation to the situation of discord in which he is placed and his inner reconciliation. The protagonist discloses himself in his inward nature because he sees himself without disguise and sees others from the same point of view. Those who, like Barker, following Bradley, concentrate upon "character", are liable to misread the plays, however, for character is exteriorization, while the plays use the outward form to disclose inner being, which is their "process and mystery".

What Professor L. C. Knights says in his entertaining *How Many Children Had Lady Macbeth* (1933) ought to be taken to heart:

> A Shakespeare play is a dramatic poem. It uses action, gesture, formal grouping and symbols, and it relies upon the general conventions governing Elizabethan plays. But, we cannot too often remind ourselves, its end is to communicate a rich and controlled experience by means of words.

A dramatic poem, to use the word of A. E., is the "most intricately organized form of thought", not a simple expression of an idea or feeling but "the greatest intensity of consciousness", and the experience intended to be communicated is, I am seeking to establish, from the example of Shakespeare, the concentrated vision of the dramatist in the terms of the leading character. Of course, what I am intending to say is much more than that drama is poetry: it is a particular kind of poetry, subject to a very firm discipline. If a sonnet has its laws, which are violated only at the certainty of disaster, so drama has its "fundamental law".

The critic who comes nearest to the perception of the law though at times making what seem to be violent departures from it is Professor G. Wilson Knight, who in a series of works devoted to the interpretation of the plays has made a contribution that is outstanding. Perhaps his most important work is *The Wheel of Fire*, and I take my quotation from the revised edition of 1949. Writing upon *Measure for Measure* he says:

> The Duke, lord of the play in the exact sense that Prospero is lord of *The Tempest*, . . . controls the action from start to finish, he allots, as it were, praise and blame, he is lit at moments with divine suggestions comparable with his almost divine power of fore-knowledge, and control and wisdom. There is an enigmatic, other worldly, mystery suffusing his figure and the meaning of his acts . . . we see the allegorical nature of the play, since the plot is so arranged that each person receives his deserts in the light of the Duke's . . . ethic.

What Professor Wilson Knight says is always true of the protagonist: as the action is in relation to him, concerns him and is his vision, he appears to control it. In this play the action springs from the Duke's will. In an imaginative and symbolic sense the protagonist creates the drama: that is to say he re-creates and re-states the situation in image, only the appearance of Nature being retained; and the art is shown in the action from first to last having relation to its end. *Measure for Measure* is tragi-comedy, so that the vision has not the sharp definition, the contrasts of light and darkness, of tragedy; instead, it has the brilliance and simultaneity, and to some extent the confusion, of dramatic action in comedy.

Commenting on two of the tragedies, Professor Knight says:

> *Othello* is dominated by its protagonist. Its supremely beautiful effects of styles are all expressions of Othello's personal passion.

> The *Macbeth* universe is woven in a texture of a single pattern. The whole play is one swift act of the poet's mind.

These remarks are what I would have him say, though I do not care for the word "dominated". The protagonist is central, the play is his, but he cannot in this or any play be said to dominate, because he is detached from the events in which he appears: in life he may have dominated, not in contemplation.

Finally Professor Knight proves that he has more than a glimpse of the law, for he says this of Macbeth:

> . . . we can say that the whole Macbeth universe reflects the mental experience of the protagonist—a technical device to make us feel his personal experience.

The idea could not be expressed better; for the personal experience of the hero imaginatively presented is exactly what Macbeth is and the other plays, too. Unfortunately, however, Professor Knight is in a difficulty about the central characters, for he finds three protagonists in Othello, Othello, Iago and Desdemona, three in King Lear, Lear, Cordelia and Edmund, and three in his favourite Timon of Athens, Timon, Apemantus and "the love of Timon". In another place he calls the third protagonist in Timon "mankind, the bride of his soul". To give a play three protagonists or any number save one is to destroy its unity: there is no work of art. Surely Professor Knight must seriously reconsider his interpretation if he finds it necessary to think of more than one leading character. In the three plays mentioned there is no difficulty whatever in distinguishing the leading character. What decides the matter is the answer to the question, Whose is the problem? The answer settles whose play it is. King Lear is concerned with Lear's fatal problem; the fact that there are other human beings in the situation with their own individual problems does not concern the dramatic action except in relation to the central problem, which is devoted to the presentation of the tremendous vision of Lear's situation from the point of view of its sublime end. Othello is Othello, no one exists in the play apart from relation to him. Iago was an upstart Renaissance young man, callous and unscrupulous, Desdemona a wilful but innocent young girl; in Othello's eyes Iago was a monster of evil, Desdemona an angel of purity. It is the enlargement of these characters in Othello's mind that makes them dramatically important, and to allow them importance in themselves is to unbalance the play. The same may be said of the other play, though Professor Wilson Knight's attempt in Timon to elevate an abstract idea into the semblance of a protagonist in so concrete a work is strange. This attitude of mind causes him to say:

> Othello's figures are first men and women, and only second symbols; the plot is first a story, second a philosophic argument. In Timon of Athens the reverse obtains. Timon is first a symbol, second a human being; the play is primarily an argument or parable, only secondarily

forced, as it best may, to assume some correspondence with the forms and events of human affairs.

The figures in fact are men and women; they become symbols in Othello's mind, in which the drama is created, and are represented by real men and women in the action of the play upon the stage, for that is the method of drama; the same is true of *Timon*. In discussing *Hamlet*, Professor Knight shows how well he sees where the drama lies, for he says of Hamlet: "He is more than protagonist: he is a play in himself". Hamlet is, indeed, the play. That is the point I am making, though I do not think a protagonist can be more than a protagonist.

Professor Arthur Sewell in *Character and Society in Shakespeare* (1951), considers that "the transformation of moral vision into dramatic form . . . is the primary business of the dramatist"; dramatic form being a work in which desires are shown in action and judged, while "the judgement is in the act of vision". But Professor Sewell does not see the vision as the protagonist's, he thinks it may be contained also in minor characters. The object of character in drama is, he thinks, to express a vision of moral actuality. Thus he sees *Hamlet* as "not the study of man, but the study of the moral nature of a man in his traffic with the outer world". I find Professor Sewell to be possibly sympathetic with the critical view I am putting forward.

On this matter of vision, Patrick Cruttwell remarks in his interesting book, *The Shakespeare Moment* (1954), that "when the heroes (or villains) of the contemporary theatre came to their ends, the Flamineos and Bosolas and Hamlets seem, at least—seem to themselves—to see things truly, and understand their lives at the moment of death". That is to get very near to what I am saying, which is that the heroes, though not the villains, do understand themselves at the moment of death when their problem is resolved and that it is from their point of view at that moment that the drama is presented.

In one of the most acute recent studies, Mr. Brents Stirling (*Unity in Shakespearean Tragedy*, 1956) suggests that "from the play, certainly not from the insight of its hero, comes significant truth"; that is, he finds unity in the play, in its ritualistic form, rather than in the protagonist. He says further:

> As we follow the protagonists in their fated careers a common quality of withdrawal into self seems to distinguish them.

That, indeed, is true; but the withdrawal is not, as he says, "always wilful or perverse", because their tragedy is in their "flawed stature", but because, I suggest, the self in its relation with the world and its inner Self, is the content of drama. Mr. Brent finds it possible to have more than one protagonist in a play (e.g. *Anthony and Cleopatra*).

Another writer on the seven tragedies, Mr. John Holloway (*Story of the Night*, 1961) refers to:

> the wholly distinctive prominence of the central character . . . what distinguishes the whole pattern of development embodied in their experiences, their whole ordeal of action and suffering.

That is the point of view I am proposing here.

It might be appropriate in closing this all too brief section upon critical discourse upon Shakespeare to draw attention to remarks of two writers not themselves Shakespearean scholars or writers upon drama that seem to have bearing upon my subject. First the philosopher Soren Kierkegaard, whose interest in drama was intense and arose out of his view of life and art (and who made a drama of his own life, which has impressed our age more, perhaps, than any contemporary drama), in a preliminary to a long account and analysis of Mozart's *Don Juan* (*Either/or*, 1843; English translation 1944), said this, which reaches, I think, the heart of the subject:

> In a drama the chief interest quite naturally centres around what one calls the hero of the play; the other characters in relation to him have only a subordinate and relative existence. The more the inward reflection penetrates the more the subordinate characters tend to assume a certain relative absoluteness. . . .
>
> The dramatist will succeed only to the degree in which nothing of the incommensurable remains, nothing of the mood from which the drama originates, that is to say, nothing of the mood *qua* mood, but in which everything is converted into the sacred dramatic coin: action and situation.
>
> If I were to characterize in a single word the effect of the drama, in so far as this is different from the effect which every other kind of poetry produces, then I should say: the drama operates in the contemporary. In the drama I see the factors standing outside one another, together in the situation, a unity of action. The more, then, the individual factors are separated, the more profoundly the dramatic situation is self-reflective, the less will the dramatic unity manifest itself as a mood, the more it will become a definite idea.

Here, in his characteristic manner, the philosopher perceives the drama in "inward reflection", which is what is contained in my definition, the inward reflection of the hero. Actuality is converted into images of action and situation. What Kierkegaard means by "the drama operates in the contemporary" is that it operates in the present moment, at the moment of presentation, not at the moment of natural time, which is an important idea. When we see a play we are offered the truth as it were at the moment of revelation. The actor presents as it were the flesh and blood of the character, and we see into the inner man at the very moment of the crisis. We get, that is to say, a vision in which we are invited to participate. Kierkegaard does, I think, put into his own philosophical language, which is his own poetic expression, the idea I have been trying to convey as to the nature of Shakespeare drama.

There is also a likeness between what I have been saying about the vision contained in drama and what the Jewish scholar, Martin Buber, writes about the saga of Moses in his book of that name, *Moses*, London, 1954). He says the saga is "not a mere recasting of the event perceived by imagination made paramount; the experience itself is creative". What Buber means is that the poetic statement in saga is not a re-telling or even an interpretation of the events, but the thing as it is actually seen at the moment of telling. In my own words, the immediacy of drama is in the protagonist's vision.

To put it in a single paragraph, it is the release from ego-centricity accomplished in the dramatic action that causes the drama to be so valuable an experience.

It should be clear that I am attempting no more than a preliminary statement of a conception of drama that deserves extended study, and upon which light may be thrown by what many writers have said or hinted at who were not themselves critics of drama. Yet it is in dramatic works themselves that most light is to be found.

DID SHAKESPEARE KNOW WHAT HE WAS DOING?

To return, therefore, to the plays. The question arises, Is it possible to suppose that Shakespeare intended to observe the principle of drama I have indicated? The answer is that he intended to write drama and that it is possible to discover what he understood drama to be by an examination of his work. The Greek dramatists did not write as they did because they had read Aristotle. It was the other way about. Aristotle wrote because he knew the Greek plays. The classical dramatists perceived the limits and specific purpose of drama. They wrote out of the tradition of Greek dramatic poetry, the single actor, the chorus, the myths of gods and heroes, and the religious ritual of public festival to which the drama belonged. Shakespeare wrote for the theatre of his own time with perception that was akin to that of the Greeks. His work will disclose to us whether he was a natural writer, a story-teller in dialogue, a mere versifier, a romanticist, one who set out to give the public what it wanted, or a dramatist who knew what he was doing in writing plays.

What is relevant in the intention of an artist is often discussed, some critics refusing to separate the work from the artist, seeing himself and his life in it, others refusing to see the artist, only the work. While I think the artist's intention to be all-important, I do not deny that his work points to himself or that it is possible to discover the artist in it, for the work contains the image, the reality or truth or beauty with which the artist is possessed. We certainly see Shakespeare in his plays : it is true that he gave himself away, and "unlocked his heart" (as all artists do); but the natural man appears always to be transformed; that is why Shakespeare is a sphinx. The attempt to attach his character and the situations in the plays to persons or events of his time is dangerously misleading. Certainly Shakespeare was affected by contemporary political and social conditions and by what happened to and around him, his up-bringing, marriage, love-affairs, work in the theatre, companions, as well as by his ambitions, successes and failures; but those accidents of time suffered transformation through his creative energy, through his imaginative vision, and became events of eternity. In the transmutation of ecstasy in the poet's mind, the facts become unrecognizable and unimportant and are not intended to be distinguished.

That the protagonist is the dramatist's mouthpiece is true, but there is no need to identify the dramatist, as a man, with him. It is not necessary to suppose that Shakespeare in his natural life was Hamlet, or Othello, or Macbeth. Certainly every character existed in the natural Shakespeare but they became his dramatic ideas. Drama was Shakespeare's concern not philosophy or history, not politics, not even the characters as such, and certainly not autobiography. Truly it is Shakespeare speaking when the characters speak, but they speak in their names, not his, through their imagined minds, not his, and the voices are their echoing words not his disguised speech. The vision is Shakespeare's, but his art makes it Hamlet's, or Othello's, or Macbeth's. "The power of the masters is shown by their self-annihilation," said Ruskin. The truth is as Shakespeare sees it, but he the man removes himself while he invites attention to it as Hamlet's, or Othello's, or Macbeth's. Through the actor who embodies the character and speaks the words, the dramatist is doubly removed; for there is first the character, next the actor. We get no nearer to the dramatist than that. And it will not do, either, as so many have attempted, to refuse to accept the play from the actor and to read the words for oneself in the isolation of one's own room, for then we get less than Shakespeare, whose intention was that the actor should offer himself "as if" he were the character: readers have no way of making up for the loss of the actor's contribution.

That Shakespeare intended to write as he did is flatly denied by Professor Wilson Knight, who will not have it that the dramatist's intentions have anything to do with the matter:

> The intentions of the artist are but clouded forms, which if he attempts to crystallize them in consciousness, may prefigure a quite different reality from that which eventually emerges in his work.

He thinks the poet writes by "instinctive power", "unknowable by intellect and intractable to memory"; we have to "submit ourselves with the utmost passivity" so that we may enter into the "original poetic experience". This appears to follow the lead of analytical psychology which finds the creative element in the sphere of the unconscious. Certainly genius is in the unconscious, but I think the creative man in his work is conscious, for the creative principle is wakefulness not sleep: as Coleridge said, "the great poet is self-conscious to a high degree". This creative consciousness is certainly not that of every-day (which is, indeed, a kind of dream), but is more rightly to be described as vision. In vision the poet discovers the unity between conscious and unconscious. He finds himself to be an instrument of the self that has consciousness of reality. Thus the poet is a transfigured man.

I should call it the poet's "awareness" rather than "intention"; awareness of the outer and inner worlds which the poet sees to be one. This awareness is what gives significance to his work and from it arises our joy in it. For the poet invites us to share actively not passively in his intended result. We are concerned, however, only with the work, not with what the poet might say about it, and any declared "intention" we are entitled to ignore. Plato long ago pointed out that what poets say about their own work can be disregarded. What the poet has to say he says in his work or not at all, and if his intention as the work discloses it is not fulfilled, he fails, no matter what he says. Professor Knight connects intentions with "sources", I do not know why. What he calls the plays' "burning central core", and their "imaginative secret" I call *meaning*. Later, Professor Knight applies intention not to the poet but to the play—"I will not say what the poet 'intended', but what the work of art itself intends", he says, as though the play writes itself.

We are not concerned with what was going on in the mind of Shakespeare at the time of writing, what he was suffering, or what he had been reading, or what his friends had said or done, or whether he wrote according to a formula, only with the work itself. How or by what Shakespeare's imagination was kindled is not our concern : we are required to give attention only to the purpose disclosed in the plays. The poet himself is not to be questioned, only his work. "The Germans," said Goethe, "ask what idea I meant to embody in my *Faust*: as if I knew myself, and could inform them", which is what all artists say. If the idea cannot be got from the work, it cannot be got at all, and unless the play informs those who receive it, what the dramatist says is irrelevant. The act of dramatic composition is that of preparation for communication, and the dramatist must intend it and bring it about. In *Sophocles the Dramatist*, Professor A. J. A. Waldock remarks that, in *Hamlet*, "make what efforts we will, we still feel at the end an uncertainty, for in that play there are suggestions of meaning not fully worked out in the action . . . there would be only one way to know and that would be to get Shakespeare and ask him". Could that be done, and were Shakespeare to answer, it would be equivalent to declaring his play a failure; for unless the play contains its own answer, the author's intention has not been fulfilled.

I do not question that the poet writes spontaneously, as though he cannot help writing, but, working by intuition, his specific task as an artist is to keep firm control upon form. Though the poet behaves as if he were irresponsible, he is not. What he cannot help is the urge, the creative energy, not the thing he does—that he chooses. And what he chooses is the form. Shakespeare chose to write plays.

B*

From a rational point of view art is an impossibility, for it is a glimpse of eternity, which by definition cannot be known in time. A Shakespeare play is a vision, and what the audience shares is vision in that particular form.

We are bound to ask what Shakespeare's plays mean. I think that what I call the law of drama enables us to see that they are symbols of human experience, which includes wonder and awe, expressed in the terms of the vision of a protagonist. The symbol transmits the experience through the performance on the stage.

This does not mean that there is no more uncertainty, for constantly we find ambiguity, which often seems to be deliberate. The dramatist chooses a double meaning, he too may be misleading, for the sake of the echoing reactions he seeks to arouse. To suppose that it is possible to arrive at the meaning of a play by a simple logical process, or superficial perception, or a single performance, is to undervalue the work. With many plays by many dramatists a single glance will indeed tell us everything. Not so with Shakespeare. The uncertainty, what may be called the unclarity, of many of the plays, the shimmer of mist that lies over them, belongs not simply to their unfading charm, but to their dramatic essence. There is everything to marvel at, interaction of mysteries, contradictions, diversion of darkness and light, juxtaposition of sublimity and comic obscenity, the whole is beyond calculation. What the dramatist seeks to establish is the hidden rhythm, the unseen flow of fullness of imagination that only the perceptive mind can understand and the sympathetic heart feel. The question always remains, what is hidden in the play? And the mystery is never cleared up, even when we think we understand.

Whether Shakespeare knew what I call the fundamental "law" of drama there is no means of telling apart from the plays, and I think they are sufficient to show that he did. It was not necessary that he should recognize a theory, but that he should perceive the essence of it in intuition and observe it as a dramatic necessity. That he did so constitutes his dramatic genius. What distinguishes a dramatist from those writers who for the life of them cannot write a play is that he possesses what Somerset Maugham calls a "knack". That is what I mean, only I call it, judging by Shakespeare, the inner recognition of a law. It is true that this knack, or intuition, or genius can be described as no more than a "knack" in most practising dramatists, for so far as my observation goes when I have discussed it with any of them I have found none to have any idea of its existence; they know only that they can write what are accepted as plays, and it is a fact that sometimes they do not know the characters they have made the protagonists in their own plays! This is unconscious writing, if you like. It is idle to speculate about Shakespeare. We have his plays, and, as he perfected his art, the recognition of the law becomes more and more definite, as we shall see.

There is surprise that Shakespeare was not recognized as superior to all other Elizabethan and Jacobean dramatists in his own time. To us his genius seems so obvious that we wonder his contemporaries did not perceive it. True, we have Jonson's testimony that he wrote for all time, and there are the praises of others, but they do not raise the recognition of his plays to a pinnacle that o'ertops the rest. The truth is that Shakespeare was doing something entirely new. Doubtless he got the impulse or direction from Marlowe, but he followed and perfected it. With him we are in a different world from that of Jonson, Chapman, Middleton or Fletcher. The fact was doubtless noted by them, and, as always, the new was not acceptable. He seems to have been regarded as above the heads of people, including the actors, demanding more than they were accustomed to give. That his plays were sufficiently popular to make him a rich man, we know; but there is a great silence that will never be broken.

There is not a scrap of evidence that Shakespeare explained what he was doing. Had he been a Bernard Shaw we should have volumes of explanation longer than the plays! But, in truth, should we? Shaw's floods of explanation are about other matters, and when he refers to his dramatic method his words have to be received with caution. His plays speak for themselves, despite the voluminous prefaces, and to understand them is to see that he took Shakespeare as his model. I conclude with some words from George Sampson (*Seven Essays*, 1947):

> The opinion of an artist about his own work has no value; the work must be transmitted and the present or future public will deliver judgement.

We can feel certain that Shakespeare would not have helped us to answer our question, and we must look at the plays for ourselves.

SHAKESPEARE'S DEVELOPMENT

That Shakespeare developed in his art no one doubts. The plays are the developments in the thought and feeling of the dramatist, and it is impossible to read them in the order in which we suppose they may have been written without getting a sense of continuity, without following the movement of a single mind, and without the conviction of a climax to the poet's life. The plays do not stand alone and ought not to be judged in isolation, but as a whole and as a single work, which has been admirably put by Mr. Eliot in his essay on John Ford:

> We may say confidently that the full meaning of any one of his plays is not in itself alone, but in that play in the order in which it was written, in relation to all his other plays, earlier and later: we must know all of his work in order to know any of it.

What is most remarkable in Shakespeare is the consistency of his work from start to finish.

There appears to be no difficulty in seeing that the plays show development when we read them bearing in mind the fundamental law. This becomes more and more perceptible in the first nine plays, between *Henry VI* (1591) and *Love's Labour's Lost* (1593); in the following ten plays, from *Romeo and Juliet* (1594) to *As You Like It* (1599), it seems to have been consciously experimented with. It is fully developed in the third group of thirteen plays, from *Julius Caesar* (1599) to *Timon of Athens* (1607), while in the final five plays, *Pericles* (1608) to *Henry VIII* (1613) the law was, with the exception of the first mentioned, taken for granted.

Shakespeare's genius is displayed in the co-ordination of his work. To slight the early plays because of their too-close likeness to the contemporary drama is to be deprived of the pleasure of observing how perfection grew. Though the youthful works were not perfect there is nothing to set beside them, not even the best of Marlowe; for they possess unmistakable signs of endeavour continued, strengthened, and made marvellously productive. From this point of view, *Henry VI* as history, *Titus Andronicus* as tragedy, and the imitations of Italian comedy have importance. Shakespeare was doing something in them, his original genius appears, and these plays would have to be recognized as remarkable, even strange, works had he done no more.

Take *Titus Andronicus*, which many critics will not have to be
Shakespeare at all. We can suppose it to be a young man's play,
written to please the actors and the audience, with the mighty and
bloody Tamberlaine in mind, but *Titus* has a definite tragic idea. We
should observe that the central character behaves in an elementary
sense as a protagonist. He appears in the first scene, and his appearance is prepared for:

> Renowned Titus, flourishing in Armes.

He is a victorious soldier; but old. The play is concerned with the
evil that befalls him by his own ruthlessness and folly. It is so constructed, however, that the protagonist is not made sufficiently
central, he is off the stage far too much, and the action is not
consistently related to him. Thus the play tends not to make sense
and is to be regarded as a failure, being too much narrative and too
little re-creation or vision. All the same, its Shakespearean quality is
unmistakable. No other dramatist could have written the play, and
while in glory of verse it is below *Tamberlaine*, in dramatic energy,
range, and purpose it is immeasurably superior.

Because the plays that immediately follow are comedies the
presence of the "law" is not easily observed, for dramatic action in
comedy is more complex than in tragedy, but a little study will show
it to be unmistakably there. I do not intend to follow its development at the moment as that will be done when we consider the
individual plays.

I note however that in all his plays Shakespeare had only three
women protagonists, in *As You Like It*, *Twelfth Night*, and *All's
Well that Ends Well*.

It appears to me that apart from the first three chronicle plays
there are three only in which the "law" is not observed, *A Midsummer Night's Dream* (1595), *The Merry Wives of Windsor* (1600),
and *Pericles* (1608). All these works are to be regarded as entertainments rather than drama. The first seems to have been written for a
wedding, and has the characteristics of a masque; the second is also
unmistakably an entertainment, a non-serious work, in which Shakespeare shows his true opinion of Falstaff; the third is a popular entertainment, a version of a well-known story, written after the great
tragedies. None has a protagonist, though Pericles is designed on the
necessary scale. Each is excellent of its kind, the first, perfect as poetry,
the second, supreme as nonsense, the third, a splendid adventure tale.

In each of the other plays, the "law" of drama can be recognized, and from *As You Like It* onwards it provides their structural discipline. This will be seen when the plays come to be studied one by one. We shall see what makes the leading character a dramatic hero is not that he suffers or is highly renowned and successful, but that he meditates upon his life, so that the play, whether comedy or tragedy, contains the fruits of reflection. The leading character moves through the action as in a dream, and when as sometimes happens the secondary characters appear more real than he, he presents them in dream. What we should look for is the ecstasy of the leading character at the climax. Ecstasy is always present in a moment that is eternity.

We shall note, too, that the tragedies are hymns in praise of life; those who see in the death of the tragic heroes or in the bloodshed that surrounds them a longing for death do the plays injustice, for they misunderstand the dramatic motive. Their tenor is freedom : the soul free from its chains, relieved of its burdens. In the Epilogue to *The Tempest*, placed first in the First Folio, the dramatist's aim is given a positive declaration :

> Gentle breath of yours, my Sailes
> Must fill, or else my project failes,
> Which was to please : Now I want
> Spirits to enforce : Art to inchant,
> And my ending is despaire,
> Unless I be reliev'd by praier
> Which pierces so, that it assaults
> Mercy itselfe, and frees all faults.

Shakespeare was a philosopher, in the sense that every great artist is a philosopher, for he knew that he meant something; and what his philosophy was can be traced in his thoughts about religion, politics and life as expressed in his works. It is not our present task to follow the course of his intellectual and spiritual growth, though that can be done.

As we read the plays one after the other we see how Shakespeare takes the familiar and transforms it into novelty. Over his work is the freshness of the newborn. Surprise is the primary emotion with which his work is received, for one did not suppose that any man had so much blood in him or such abysses of spirit. Why Shakespeare chose the themes upon which he wrote is a legitimate question but only the plays can answer it. He chose them because he thought the themes important and because he thought he could make plays out of them. A dramatist in the full tide of creative energy is not short of themes, however, and does not have to search for them. They are wherever he casts his eye, in his contacts with men, in his own heart and mind. He has affinity with the world, sympathy, sensitiveness, and poetic insight. All these qualities were brought together in Shakespeare, and if there is one thing more certain than another it is his abounding fertility.

So long as man is contained upon the earth the truth of Shakespeare's works will endure. It is impossible that the plays should become stale, for their material is the imperfection of man, upon which the light of an all-seeing eye and all-understanding mind is thrown, and the multiplying evils of existence are embraced in a comprehending vision in which chaos is resolved, the heart quietened, and order restored. This sense of order is Shakespeare's supreme contribution to human well-being. He is of the earth and misses nothing of human weakness, folly and wickedness, not a jot of the inexplicable accumulation of error and sin is evaded, yet the conviction of the continuity of purpose, of truth, goodness, and beauty as the goal of existence is unmistakable. Beyond all the vagaries of human thought about the situation of man there is in Shakespeare the recognition of providence, of divinity, that pervades the whole of life. His drama lies in the inner truth or harmony of the divine-human world. His recurrent theme is the waywardness of the human heart, which in a subtle way he shows to be a reflection of the apparent waywardness in the heart of Being. The likeness between man and God is startlingly revealed in their joint purposes, so that in Shakespeare's world everything is kin, the world all of a piece, and man and God in final harmony. That is why his plays give such inexhaustible satisfaction and we see them over and over again without getting wearied. That is why he wrote for all time and for all people, not as an Englishman for the English simply, but with the pen of a divine being delineating the drama of mankind. Shakespeare's plays are the equivalent in the adult world of the nursery tales that can be repeated endlessly to children. They are eternal.

PART II

Upon Shakespeare Interpretation

THE SHAKESPEARE STAGE

I ADD a few notes upon the more obvious implications of the recognition of the "law" of drama upon the interpretation of the plays. In the first place it has bearing upon their staging, and an important change is indicated in the practice of acting that has persisted since the Restoration, also in the naturalistic and spectacular adaptation of the plays to the requirements of the picture-frame stage to which actors and producers have been restricted for more than a hundred years.

Practically all Shakespeare scholarship has had the picture-frame stage in mind, and the plays have been judged as drama from what is thought to be suited to that stage. Although a change is taking place in the attitude of scholars, only too often the Shakespeare stage is still regarded as an imperfect form of ideal stage, and it is considered to be a help to the dramatist for editors to bring the plays into conformity with an imaginary ideal not far removed, in fact, from a perfected picture-frame stage. It seems to me, however, from my own experience and studies that unless the text is regarded in its relation to the principle of the Shakespeare stage, and what the dramatist is aiming at on that stage is understood, the risk of serious misinterpretation and when they come to be produced the sacrifice of the plays to fancies of producers are both unavoidable.

I am not intending to suggest that the plays require a reconstruction of the Elizabethan stage. There is still much dispute about that stage, and the settlement of the questions that arise are of historical interest, but their practical significance is small. So long as it is understood that what the actor needs is a stage upon which the protagonist can fulfil his function, the form of the stage is secondary. When the stage is looked at from the point of view of the actor, and when what the actor does is subject to the requirements of the "law" of drama, the plays will be presented in the sense with which they were written. The actor and his audience should determine the form of the theatre and its stage, not the styles, methods or ambitions of producers or designers.

What the actor offers is the concrete experience of human knowledge, and the deliverance from human woes in the terms of drama. All art is concreteness; and the drama is the most concrete of arts because in the actors' flesh and blood the Word is made flesh. The interpretation of the plays I put forward here makes more of the stage, in the sense of making the plays directly dependent upon the actor. There is presented to the spectators, in the visual forms of princes and beggars, noble and wicked characters, their own hearts' longing for reconciliation. How important, therefore, are the stage and acting! The production of plays should be looked upon, as in ancient Athens, as a civic duty. All the arts are contained in the drama, and the city itself lives in it, for bodied forth in the play is the city's profound, complex, and creative inner life. The drama is the complete social art, for it is participated in socially, and its themes concern all men.

The function of the stage in a particular play is to recreate in the minds of the spectators the vision beheld by the dramatist. To do that, producer and actors have to enter into the vision, and themselves, by beholding, experience it. Drama is the art of communication between dramatist and spectator with the stage and the actor interposed, the dramatist eliminating himself. Drama is not a matter of theatrical incidents, however, its rationale is that it enables the dramatist to invite the spectator into a realm, elevated beyond natural life, beautiful and real, exciting, tragic or comic, containing the truth of imagination.

THE LEADING CHARACTER

It is essential to my argument that everything depends upon accepting the function of the leading character. What the play contains is to be understood first in the context of the centrality of the protagonist, not of plot, or history, or topical events, or even a psychology. When the protagonist or leading character is recognized, the direction of the play's action can be followed, and the relation of the other characters to him and to each other, and the significance of their parts in the action, can be seen. I especially invite the reader to consider what I have written about *The Merchant of Venice* where the largest and most interesting character is not the protagonist, yet the play is given its proper value only when the Merchant is recognized as the leading character; that is to say, when he is seen to be central to the action throughout. This is contrary to the usual treatment of the play, yet unless the place of Antonio is recognized the play becomes disbalanced, without focus, and the dramatic action cannot properly be carried out. Actor-managers have never thought of playing the part of the Merchant, because Shylock is so unmistakably the better part, more suitable as a vehicle for the display of personal talents. One does not question the instinct of the actor-managers or that Shylock is one of the most attractive and rewarding of parts, so long as the position of Antonio is not allowed to be overshadowed. It is the play's dramatic action that Antonio should succeed and Shylock fail, and in its performance that should be established.

More responsibility rests upon the leading character than upon any other, for the protagonist has to present the play and to be in conscious touch with the audience. His is the task of persuading the audience to participate, and unless the actor succeeds in this, not merely by the attractiveness of his personality but by the manner in which the entire dramatic action is put forward, so that the audience surrenders itself, the play fails. The protagonist enters upon the stage as the scene of his visionary experience and comes before the audience with conviction of its significance; it is he who raises the play to the level of tragic or comic intensity. The rhythm of the play is largely determined by him, and the revelation it contains is what he unfolds. It is a much more crucial function than is generally supposed in this day of emphasis upon ensemble acting.

THE SECONDARY CHARACTERS

What I have said about the leading character does not mean the belittlement of the secondary characters. Indeed, they are to be raised to the level of the leading character. Shakespeare's art is in allowing the secondary characters to appear to be speaking in their own persons, though in fact they never do, for they speak and move as the protagonist hears and sees them; yet they are made to possess the utmost verisimilitude and self-possession. Their language does not have the mere echo of the protagonist's voice, but belongs to the individual character and the situation. To achieve this in the play's writing is the task of the dramatist, and to carry it out on stage is part of the difficult art of acting; for the actor has to present a flesh and blood person in actions that have concreteness in life, yet his relation to the protagonist must be maintained, for he is not there for his own sake.

The actor-managers only too often treated the secondary characters as mere "feeds" to their own effectiveness. A position of subordination was established, and the essential part in the drama taken by these characters was often ignored, though they are as much a part of the dramatic action as the protagonist himself. To weaken them or to allow them anything less than their full value weakens the protagonist also and lowers the effectiveness of the play. There is not a single character in a Shakespeare play that is unnecessary or that can be ignored. What has to be decided is the dramatic value of the character, that is to say the value he has in the situation as presented in the protagonist's vision, and this value must be established. This, I think, gives more validity to the secondary parts than to make them dependent upon themselves, as if they were required to establish themselves on their own large or small merits. All the parts belong firmly to the whole, being constituent elements in the vision, and unless that is brought out the play is not properly performed. Those actor-managers, or producers, who give perfunctory attention to secondary characters fail in a fundamental duty to the play.

Tolstoy found fault with Shakespeare's characters for talking alike: "They all talk in the same manner . . . from the quality of the language we should be quite unable to ascertain who is speaking," he said. There is something in this, for we always hear what the protagonist causes us to hear. Yet the critics are solidly against Tolstoy, for there is nothing they are more agreed upon than that Shakespeare was a master of dramatic characterization. This also is true; for a dramatist not only seeks to make his characters convincing, to give them flesh and blood, but to put them in possession of the situations that constitute the dramatic action: dramatic characterization being the creation of characters concerned with action. Therefore the people of the play are re-created in imagination, and presented in the protagonist's terms, larger, greater, meaner, more strikingly perfect or devilish than they ever were in life itself.

The secondary characters are individual, because visualized concretely, and so many-sided that occasionally one of them is mistaken for the protagonist. As they are the shadows of his thoughts, they, like shadows on a wall, may become more gigantic than he. Iago, is

an outstanding instance. Henry Arthur Jones, one of the mistaken
ones, said:

> Othello is not the protagonist of the play. Iago is the real protagonist
> as every actor who has played Othello knows.

Other examples are Juliet in *Romeo and Juliet*, Falstaff in *Henry IV*,
Angelo in *Measure for Measure*, Lady Macbeth in *Macbeth*, and
Iachimo in *Cymbeline*. These highly important, even superb or
monstrous parts, are none the less secondary, and must not be
elevated in acting to the central place, as is so often done. Iago, an
interesting villain in himself, gets all his importance from Othello,
and to think otherwise is gross misunderstanding. Every word of
Juliet's is related to Romeo. Falstaff has always the Prince in mind.
Angelo gains his significance from the Duke, who is ever present in
his thoughts. Lady Macbeth moves under the figure of her husband.
Iachimo is another villain of the Iago type. The size and strength of
these characters mean that the protagonist needs them to hold the
stage against him. For that reason, what is demanded of the actor in
secondary parts in Shakespeare must never be underestimated.

Their importance to the protagonist appears most strikingly in the
scenes in which he does not appear in person. It will be found that
these scenes do not suffer from his absence, for they are almost always
made highly vivid and possess some degree of exaggeration in action
and speech. In these scenes there is usually some relaxation of tension,
but always with relation to the dramatic action. I draw attention
to some of these scenes when commenting on the plays.

A NOTE ON COMEDY

At this point something should be said about comedy, which forms
a large part of the plays, among them the greatest comedies in the
language. Shakespeare is essentially a tragic dramatist, so that his
comedies have tragic undertones; none the less they are true
comedies, with joyful resolutions, *As You Like It* and *Twelfth Night*,
in particular, being as near perfection as a man's work can reach.
In tragedy the centrality of the hero is easily perceived, but in comedy
the protagonist cannot always be recognized at once. Indeed it is
sometimes supposed that comedy needs two or more leading
characters, or, indeed, none at all; but if what I have called the

fundamental law of drama is a "law" at all, it must apply to comedy equally with tragedy. A comedy has one protagonist, who presents the play, whose vision constitutes the drama, and who functions exactly as in tragedy. When we examine the plays it will be seen that in this sense there is no difference between the two categories of plays. Indeed, the same is true of tragi-comedy, of which there are several examples in Shakespeare, also of farce, of which there are no examples, the nearest being, perhaps, *The Comedy of Errors*. Comedy is sometimes regarded as inferior to tragedy, which would be true if the law did not apply to it; but the masks of Thespis look in opposing ways at the same time; comedy is as much a part of human existence as tragedy and is to be treated with as much respect. As the aim of tragedy is to purify by suffering so comedy purifies by laughter. In tragedy the greatness of man is the theme, his fall, and how he rises again; in comedy the theme is the folly of man, and how he may be saved from its consequences.

THE PLAYS' MEANING

The foregoing are the considerations that should be uppermost when the reader sets out to understand the plays, and when producers and actors prepare to perform them. The protagonist has to be recognized and given the central position, the action has to be seen to be the working out of his problem, and the secondary characters have to be given their place in relation to him. Whenever the protagonist appears he decides the centre of interest, for the play is his life's vision. The composition of the stage pictures are determined by this fact, and the position of the actors must be carefully thought out in relation to it. There is no exception to this rule. That is why drama is a difficult and complex art; those who deny it do so in an effort to make drama easier than it ever can be for actors and audience, as well as for readers.

Though we cannot deny that a play as it appears on the stage is body, it is not mere body, and by relying upon pleasing the eye and gratifying the scenes the essential meaning of drama is lost. As Henry James said as an exasperated playlover:

> The more it is painted and dressed, the more it is lighted and furnished and solidified, the less it corresponds or coincides, the less it squares with our imaginative habits.

Unless the play as produced is treated as symbol, that is, as a work of imagination, it fails. This, actors and producers enamoured of actual life, which is so much easier than imagination, only too often forget. Thus, throughout the nineteenth century, and in the first fifty years of the twentieth, the false approach to the plays that first Lamb condemned, and afterwards Henry James castigated in almost identical words, has continued. Yet producers still put themselves before the plays, and encourage actors to put themselves before their parts. What the play means is seldom asked, and the attempt is made to get novelty, to be startling, and to overwhelm the audience with display. Cutting is still practised mercilessly, and scenes are transposed as it suits the producer. This happens because there is no recognized law of drama in accordance with which the production needs to be carried out and by which it is to be judged. Plato's famous analogy of the bed (in the *Republic*) that there is the idea of the bed, the actual bed, and what the painter makes of it, which led him to condemn the poetic dramatist for imitating imitations, is a condemnation stage producers often should feel.

What happens before the action opens, and what follows its completion, have nothing to do with the play. There is no need to visualize the characters, even the leading character, in any earlier situation, for the play contains everything essential to the drama. Therefore there is no need to probe into history or origins, any more than there is need to consider what happened after the action is over. Even to raise these questions is a sign that the play's meaning is not appreciated, or perhaps that the dramatist himself has failed. Shakespeare does not point either before or after; his works are complete in themselves.

"The play is the idea," said Gordon Craig, whose aim was to practise what he called "the art of the theatre", by which he meant a drama dependent upon a theatre in which music, painting, architecture, poetry were to be transformed into a different art. But Craig was emphatic upon respecting the work of the dramatist, though it is true that he wrote at times as though the dramatist were unnecessary. What he meant was that the dramatist ought to be a member of an acting company, working on the stage with actors, as Shakespeare did, otherwise he comes in as a stranger. With that I think we must at least have sympathy, for to carry out what Craig demanded we should have to return to the conditions of Shakespeare's theatre. Yet it is none the less true that the dramatist as such disappears from the stage set for his play, though he makes everything else possible, for without the idea there is no drama, he leaves the task of its unfolding to the actor, the true master of the art of the theatre. This should be recognized in the production of Shakespeare. What is the idea in the play? is the first question to be asked and answered, for the idea is nothing less than the reason for the play's existence. To the exposition of that answer the actor and director must devote themselves.

What is the dramatic idea? It is not the plot, or the scenes, or the characters. It is always in the problem of the leading character and how that problem is resolved—that is to say, in the dramatic action. There is no need to look for any other governing idea in Shakespeare, for, as long as the theatre lasts, to give expression to that idea the skill, energy, knowledge and imaginative powers of every director and actor will be called for. Whether the play is comic, even farcical, or whether it is tragedy, even tragi-comedy, the dramatic idea is the resolution of the confusions and conflict of human life through order, expressed in reconciliation. Shakespeare perceived history, politics, human relations, quarrels, personal ambitions and love as the background of the spiritual drama, and the spiritual drama as the ultimate truth of man.

SPEAKING THE VERSE

One of the practical questions for the actor is the verse. How it was spoken on Shakespeare's stage we do not know, for Elizabethan pronunciation was not the same as ours, and were we to hear Elizabethan actors speak it is likely that we should not understand them. We have the plays, however, and the spelling and punctuation of the original texts, so that without being pedantic or antiquarian it is possible by observing them to get an idea not of how the plays were said but of how they might still be said. By doubling the consonants, by extending vowels, sometimes by the contractions of words, as well as by the form of the verse, the lines may be spoken with something of their full meaning, as can be discerned by practice. Above everything, if the qualities of the verse itself be recognized, both blank verse and rhymed, also the rhythm of the prose speeches, a secure approach to the sense of the plays will be made. Indeed, rhythm, cadence, melody, incantation, declamation, and every kind of rhetorical device are to be found in them, and the last thing to be heard is the casual tones of conversation in ordinary life.

Until the verse is mastered, the characters cannot truly be played. As a visual art the drama is intended for the eye, but it is equally addressed to the ear, and wrong speaking distorts the play. The language of Shakespeare decides not only how the actor speaks but what he does and where he stands. Therefore to speak the lines for sense, having looked for what is called the "key" word, is the exact opposite to what is required, for the sense escapes the speaker unless the verse itself is understood. This means that in blank verse the line must be recognized with its stresses, which vary continually. Only when that is done does the sense appear. I am not suggesting that nothing but the rhythm of the verse needs to be mastered, for the actor must understand what he is saying: too many actors appear to be unconscious of the meaning of the words they utter; but line, stresses and meaning are one, and are to be taken together. The importance of this is that the dramatic action is contained in the verse, for that is the essential nature of dramatic poetry.

Each different kind of speech in the plays has to be said with under-standing of its nature. There are (a) soliloquies, spoken with no other character present, (b) monologues, consisting of reflections, apostrophes, invocations, or denunciations, spoken in the presence of others and heard by them, (c) sentences or monologues, which others on the stage are not supposed to hear, sometimes called "asides", (d) dialogue that in form is addressed to another character but is in the nature of declamation or exclamation, and (e) straight dialogue addressed to other characters and spoken directly to them. These different kinds of speech often occur in the same play, sometimes there are several changes in the same scene, even more than one change may take place in the same speech.

Almost invariably the long speeches, and the soliloquies always, are intended to be addressed to the audience for the sake of bringing it directly into the action. This is not done in Shakespeare's plays in the manner Quiller-Couch supposed (*Shakespeare's Workmanship*, 1918):

> . . . a player who had some specially fine passage to declame advanced and began, laying his hand to his heart—
> > All the world's a stage. . . .
> or
> > The Quality of Mercy is not strained. . . .

or (raising his hand to his brow)
> To be, or not to be, that is the question. . . .

and, having delivered himself, pressed his hand to his heart again, bowed to the discriminating applause, and retired into the frame of the play.

The actor does not step out of the frame, because there is no frame to step out of, and nothing of the kind is intended. Quiller-Couch was so persuaded of the merits of the early twentieth century picture stage, with its "straight-drawn front, with footlights", that he was for ever sympathizing with Shakespeare over the supposed defects of the Elizabethan stage! It is true that the Elizabethan audience listened for rhetorical displays, and applauded them, and it is true, as we know, that on the eighteenth-century picture stage actors did step out of the play to make their personal display. That, of course, should be made unnecessary. These rhetorical speeches are an essential part of the Shakespeare play, written for delivery in the course of its action, carrying the action forward, which the open stage allowed to be done. The plays were written for a stage on which the actor knew how to speak to the audience throughout his performance, and at the same time to speak in the play. This is an art our actors have to re-learn, if they are to play Shakespeare correctly.

An object of the soliloquy is the self-exposure of the speaker. It is not mere thinking aloud. The audience is directly addressed and taken straight into the character's confidence. Schueckling and others have seen in it as used on the picture stage one "among the naive devices used for enlightening the audience", as though the technique of a stage in which the audience is supposed not to be there were superior, more intelligent, even more dramatic than that of Shakespeare's stage. The supposition is ill-founded. Shakespeare's way was better not worse than that to which we are accustomed. Dramatic skill is understood to consist of the way in which the plot is unfolded or the characters revealed. I suggest that its secret is in the way in which the dramatist, through the protagonist, gets the audience to enter into the dramatic action. It is contained, too, in the nature of the problem; for it is not any kind of problem, but the personal problem of the protagonist, that which brings him into the conflict, which constitutes the dramatic action, and though many problems may be raised in a play, *all* other problems must have bearing upon the central problem.

It should be noted that soliloquies in Shakespeare are almost invariably spoken by the protagonist, Iago being an exception, Iachimo another, both secondary characters, both villains and much alike, whose soliloquies reveal their aims in relation to the protagonist, and may be understood as continuations of his own speech. Lady Macbeth also has a number of such speeches, and in them we should hear the echo of the hero's thoughts. In the early *Two Gentlemen of Verona* several characters beside the protagonist soliloquize.

Monologues, distinguished from soliloquies because there are other characters present who hear what is said, have much the same object as the soliloquy, though a double object, and are difficult for actors brought up on the picture-stage. "Asides" should be spoken not in the air, to nobody, but directly to and looking at the audience. Another kind of speech presenting difficulty is when the character addresses others but says more than is necessary for them to hear. Straight dialogue, in the nature of conversation between characters, has to be kept on the same level as the other speeches, not lowered to that of naturalistic conversation.

What I have said here is no more than an indication of the treatment called for by the different kinds of speeches on the theory of Shakespeare drama to which I have devoted these pages; but this is not the place to give examples or to go into detail, which would require a book to itself.

Scenes usually end with couplets of rhymed verse, which should be given emphasis, not said casually as the characters move off. They are a full-close to what has gone before. Always when rhyme occurs, except in the earliest plays, it is intended to draw attention to what is said. Speaking should not be on the rhymes but on the stresses. Speech generally should be rapid, for there is usually much to get in, but there must be variations in speed, not all characters speaking alike, with the recognition of pauses and silences, all of which is highly important.

The advantage of using a Shakespeare text with the original spelling is that it is a guide to the lengthening of the vowels and prolonging the consonants. Capital initials usually indicate words to be stressed, and the original punctuation ought to be followed. As Shakespeare's plays are poems, to under-speak them or to ignore their poetry is to undervalue them, while to cut or transpose scenes does violence to the poem as well as to the dramatic action. The poem and the dramatic action are one.

THE AUDIENCE

A few words should be added upon the place of the audience from the point of view from which I am writing. The protagonist is conscious of the audience, for he presents the dramatic action for its participation. Yet in the aim to be thought natural, dramatists and actors, too, will sometimes go to any length to avoid the audience, and we have that prince of comedy-writers, Congreve, saying in the early days of the introduction of the picture frame stage, in the dedicatory epistle to *The Double-Dealer*:

> . . . in any part of a play, if there is expressed any knowledge of an audience, it is unsufferable . . . because we are concealed spectators of the plot in agitation.

As at that date the audience was not sitting in the dark but had as much light upon it as there was upon the stage, the remark is odd, and to suppose the audience to be "concealed" was to throw an impossible task upon the actor. In fact, the audience is never concealed, even in our modern darkened theatres, but does its best to be in active participation: in a sense the first member of the audience is the protagonist himself. The weight of this knowledge is thrust upon the actor, for his art is one of communication, and though he dare not be self-conscious without destroying his art, he must be conscious of the audience's presence and know that he has to communicate to it.

Audiences go to plays to be taken out of their surroundings; they are in the theatre so that the protagonist may introduce them into his world of vision. To escape from the actual world and to attain delight in the imaginary world are their desires. If it be asked what an audience should expect to get from a play, the answer is that it depends in part upon what the dramatist through the actor offers, but it also depends largely upon what the audience contributes. A detached audience gets nothing, for it enables the actors to do next to nothing. Only the collaborating audience ready to work with the actors (a more pleasant and easier kind of work than the actors are required to do, but, none the less, depending upon a disposition to participate) is rewarded. Otherwise nothing. There has to be community in an audience of participating and receiving minds. An audience of one is an impossibility. Yet it is the actor's business to

arouse the attention and sympathy of the audience that places itself
in his hands. He has to inform it of what he purposes, and by appeal
and persuasion get it to accept and act upon, mentally and emotion-
ally, what he puts before it in words and movement. To establish that
relation was Shakespeare's intention as dramatist and it is what the
actors aim at: the audience should meet them halfway. At present,
with the actor withdrawn behind the proscenium frame, and the
audience withdrawn into itself in the darkness, that is very hard.
Both actors and audience tend to concentrate upon themselves, when
their attitude should be towards each other, to effect the meeting
between them. That meeting is not personal, but a spiritual com-
munion in an object beyond themselves, for the actor invites contact
through the play, in the terms of the image he is presenting, and
the audience is looking for the experience contained in the image.
Upon the disposition of the audience to respond to the actor's
invitation everything depends.

Theatres are required that favour such a disposition. Existing
theatres do not, so that audiences are as badly handicapped as actors.
Sitting in the theatre of today audiences are reduced into passivity,
which not infrequently induces sleep. Indeed, unless kept awake by
a succession of shocks, verbal, visual or aural, they are apt to feel
done out of something: the idea that they have anything to do does
not occur to them. This points to the importance of theatre design
as a factor in the performance of Shakespeare, and in making possible
the reception of what the dramatist has to offer. Since the later
seventeenth century in England, theatre buildings have become increasingly ill-adapted to their essential purpose. Wrong theatre
construction forces an audience into a wrong relation to the play, so
that intimacy and directness of participation are impossible. Shakespeare wrote for an audience pressing upon the stage, able because
of its nearness to surrender immediately to the dramatic action under
the influence of the actor. To restore that immediate contact is
necessary, because without it the difficulty, even the impossibility,
of such exchange prevents the drama existing in its fullness.

In writing thus upon the actor and the audience I have sought to
apply what has been said in these pages upon what happens in
Shakespeare. When a Shakespeare play is recognized as essentially
an imaginative presentation from a single point of view of characters
in a human predicament, it follows that participation is invited from
that point of view. What the actor attempts and what the audience

has to do are both affected by this fact. I think it gives the plays a renewed significance, elevating the drama to its rightful level as an act of consciousness. When Shakespeare's plays are treated with respect, probed into, looked at with insight, accepted as the work of an unfailing master of dramatic truth; when no attempt is made to interpose the cleverness of producers; when the indifference of actors is removed by consciousness of their responsibilities and the sheer hardness of their task; and when the audience is enabled to take its proper part in active reception and participation, then the enrichment of our existence by the continued performance of these plays becomes one of the supreme tasks and highest delights of civilized life.

PART III

The Plays

a

CHRONOLOGY AND CLASSIFICATION

WHEN the plays of Shakespeare were written and performed is a subject on which information is meagre. The results of scholarship are approximate, and there is no final agreement, every estimate being sooner or later upset. I propose to follow in the main the chronology of Sir E. K. Chambers in his *William Shakespeare* (1932), though that scholar queried some of his own conclusions, and I am not altogether convinced by some of his reasoning in the book to which I refer. Yet Sir Edmund summarized the evidence fairly, the most important qualification to bear in mind when using the dates being that some of the plays may have been performed earlier. All, of course, were written earlier, though how much earlier we do not know.

In the First Folio of 1623 the plays were classified as Comedies, Histories and Tragedies, and this classification has since been followed in all collected editions. The order of the plays there, apart from this classification, does not appear to follow any plan. The last play but one is placed first, and the plays do not seem to be in order of performance, or composition, or preference. If there was any rule we do not know what it was.

In the following pages, I have adopted the chronological sequence, grouping the plays in periods for convenience of study. A different grouping could be adopted, and other groupings have been used by others for various purposes, while changes in the grouping would follow changes in chronology. For my purpose, however, such changes do not greatly matter, and I do not attach significance to the four groups beyond the general evidence provided of development in the observance of the law of drama; but this development was not continuous from play to play. What makes Shakespeare the master dramatist and his plays the most worth study of any dramatic works is that observing its discipline he re-creates the idea of drama and offers new possibilities of dramatic experience.

THE FIRST PERIOD
(1591-1593)

*Henry VI, Parts 2 and 3—Henry VI, Part 1—Richard III
—Titus Andronicus—The Taming of the Shrew—The
Comedy of Errors—The Two Gentlemen of Verona—Love's
Labour's Lost.*

A S I have explained, the plays have been grouped for convenience and as far as possible in the order in which they were performed, which approximates to the order in which they were written, except that the dates were earlier. Their cumulative effect will be realized when the plays are read in this order. It may generally be taken for granted that performance followed quickly after composition because the demand for new plays was great.

In the quotations from the plays I have used the original spelling, except that the long *s* is not repeated and the letter *v* is printed instead of *u*. I have also carefully followed the original punctuation, which conveys Shakespeare's meaning better than the more correct modern punctuation.

I draw special attention to the fact that in this and the following chapters I do not attempt a critique of the plays but confine myself to the specific subject of this book, which is to recognize the law of drama.

Of the first nine plays the order is very uncertain. *Titus Andronicus* may have been written earlier than 1592, and may have been preceded by *Richard III*. Either or both plays may have been written to enable Richard Burbage to compete with Edward Alleyn. It is interesting to speculate upon this subject; the facts are few. On the whole I see insufficient reason to change the accepted order. It can be said of these plays that what I have called the law of drama is only imperfectly to be recognized in them, but in all except the three *Henry VI* plays it seems to be there. There is here a group of dramatic productions over two or three years, when Shakespeare was discovering what the writing of plays demanded. They are mere hints of genius, not the works of genius itself.

THE SECOND PART OF HENRY THE SIXTH
THE THIRD PART OF HENRY THE SIXTH (1591)
THE FIRST PART OF HENRY THE SIXTH (1592)

These are generally supposed to be Shakespeare's first plays, and it is convenient to consider them as one. They are chronicles in which history is unfolded. The critics, from Theobald (1754) to Dr. Dover Wilson (1951), seem to judge them from the point of view of the later plays, and, because their quality is unequal, the characters poorly drawn, and the verse inferior, they are only too ready to doubt "whether they were entirely of his writing". This seems to me poor criticism. It is taken for granted that Shakespeare, as Dr. Dover Wilson says, spent "at least part of his early years revising or re-writing the plays of other men", but the names of great scholars do not make this anything but guesswork. Perhaps he did so, and because in these early plays there is writing inferior to his best, and, because, too, in the plays of others there is writing that is remotely like Shakespeare's, textual critics have scope for much guessing. Yet in truth there was nothing like these plays before Marlowe's Edward II, if, indeed, that play was the earlier work, which it may not have been, for Shakespeare's aim was history, not mere story-telling, the presentation of his country's not-far-distant history, and an original contribution to the theatre.

It is impossible to read them without bearing in mind the play that is immediately to follow, Richard III, the leading character of which appears in the second and third plays. And the plays written five or six years later, also, which show firmer grasp of dramatic construction, and that last of the series, in time of writing, which proves that Shakespeare knew exactly what he was doing.

Certainly, these three plays are imperfect works, which is only to be expected, but none the less they are vital, vigorous, lively, with a marked sense of acting values, for they stage well. As they give an account of the Wars of the Roses, they are full of battles. Henry VI is a baby in Part I, marries in the second part, and in the third is deposed and murdered. The problem with which the plays are concerned is who is to have the throne and rule the land. It is a political problem, not a problem of drama, for in none of the plays is there a protagonist.

THE TRAGEDY OF RICHARD III (1592)

Judging from the six Quartos published from 1597 onwards, this was a popular play. It long continued to be popular, especially after Colley Cibber "improved" it in 1700, for it contains one of the most showy parts for actors in Shakespeare. The subject matter is politics viewed in the terms of the leading character, Richard III, who is a villain. Here we have an approach to drama, for there is a protagonist with a problem; none the less the play is imperfect drama for reasons we will discuss. It is conceived as tragedy, but, despite powerful theatrical effectiveness, it fails as such; it will be worth while to consider in the light of the law of drama why that is so.

Richard, who had already appeared in the second and third parts of *Henry* VI, is unmistakably the protagonist. He opens the play, its action follows his actions, and he is killed at the end. He has the dimensions of a hero, but as he claims to be a villain, he cannot sustain the place of hero. He says at the start:

> I am determined to prove a Villaine,
> And hate the idle pleasures of these dayes.
> Plots have I laide, Inductions dangerous,
> By drunken Prophesies, Libels, and Dreames,
> To set my brother Clarence and the King
> In deadly hate, the one against the other.
>
> (1.1)

The play raises the question of the qualities required in a tragic hero and the nature of the problem with which he is concerned. Richard is a great noble, Protector of the young King, and finally King himself. He could hardly be in a more elevated position; nevertheless, as he remains a villain, relentless and immovable in his pride, and does not change, he cannot play the part of a protagonist, even though designed for it.

Villains cannot create tragedy; they provide the subject matter of stories, entertainments, or terrible or painful events, not of drama. Tragedy necessarily concerns men of elevation of mind and greatness of soul, whose problem is a moral one, who seek good, but fail because of wilful mistakes, or moral weakness, or destiny, or the hand of Providence. They fail because of some fault, or because the Universe appears to be against them. The hero presents himself on the stage, seeking the audience's participation. This does not apply to Richard. He seeks evil, and fails through the accident of battle. We are called upon to admire his courage, audacity, and unscrupulousness, but we cannot sympathize with or participate in his wickedness, for he is a man who is an unashamed murderer many times over, deceitful, unscrupulous in the highest degree, choosing evil because he rejoices in it. His physical deformity is a symbol of the deformity of his mind. He is indifferent to right and wrong, or prefers wrong because it amuses him. It is true that he is clever, audacious and courageous, and has appealing qualities of frankness, but no more. Before the final battle, he defies the natural order in the following terms:

> Give me a Kalender: Who saw the Sunne today?

> Not I my lord.

> Then he disdaines to shine: for by the Booke
> He should have brav'd the Easte an houre ago,
> A blacke day will it be to somebody. Ratcliffe.

> My lord.

> The Sun will not be seene today
> The sky doth frowne, and lowre upon our Army.
> I would these dewy teares were from the ground.
> Not shine today? Why, what is that to me
> More than to Richmond? For the selfe-same Heaven
> That frownes on me, lookes sadly upon him.
> (5.3)

This man has no comprehension of Providence. He acknowledges only his own will and interests. It is the poetical spirit with which Shakespeare endows him that gives him a deceitful romantic charm, so that when in almost his last words he says

> A thousand hearts are great within my bosom.
> (5.3)

our hearts warm to him. Yet a protagonist cannot invite an audience to participate in villainy, for to do that would make the drama an instrument of evil. Richard's problem, which is to secure the throne and keep himself there, does not make a tragic problem because it exists in immoral terms.

The play, therefore, is not tragedy and Richard's death is not a tragic end. Had the troubled conscience of Richard been allowed to change the man the result might have been different, but the conscience of Shakespeare's Richard is declared to be undisturbed. What the Second Murderer said about conscience before the murder of Clarence is to be understood as Richard's own ironic view:

> I'le not meddle with it, it makes a man a Coward: A man cannot steale, but it accuseth him: A man cannot Sweare, but it Checks him: A man cannot lye with his Neighbour's Wife, but it detects him. 'Tis a blushing shamefac'd spirit, that mutinies in a mans bosome: It fills a man full of obstacles. It made me once refuse a Purse of Gold that (by chance) I found: It beggars any man that keepes it: It is turned out of Townes and Cities for a dangerous thing, and every man that means to live well, endeavours to trust to himselfe, and live without it.
>
> (1.4)

and so he goes on. That Shakespeare's aim was to show a man indifferent to conscience we see in Richard's terrible dream:

> My Conscience hath a thousand severall Tongues,
> And every Tongue brings in a severall Tale,
> And every Tale condemnes me for a Villaine . . .

and though he admits that his dream

> Have stroke more terror to the soule of Richard
> Than can the substance of ten thousand Souldiers . . .

he boasts that he has had the sweetest sleep:

> I promise you my Heart is very jocond,
> In the remembrance of so faire a dreame . . .

and soon says:

> Let not our babling Dreames affright our soules:
> For Conscience is a word that Cowards use,
> Devis'd at first to keepe the strong in awe,
> Our strong armes be our Conscience, Swords our Law.
>
> (5.3)

The play has been called melodrama, but that is to mistake it. Melodrama is a term too freely used in criticism when a play is too difficult to categorize. It properly applies to a dramatic entertainment concerned with a simple conflict between good and evil, which ends in the victory of good, enabling actors to display themselves in striking parts without great demands upon them or taking them to the high levels of their art. This particular work is a shocker, an unpleasant play. There is no other character in Shakespeare like Richard, despite Bradley's effort, following Thomas Whately (1785), to see him in Macbeth. Richard is not a man but a monster: as he declares:

I love myself.
(5.3)

To say, as H. B. Charlton does, that "Richard is his first embodiment of the stupendous stature of the human atom. . . ." is true in the sense that the monstrous exists in the human soul, for all evil has a place in that centre of disharmony, but the monstrous does not increase the stature of the "human atom"; only enlarges its illusion. Because there is no redemption in Richard's soul, no resolution of order, but personal defeat and chaos, the play has not the dimensions of tragedy. Although written in the terms of Richard, it is a mere thriller for all its poetry. Shakespeare never wrote another play like it; it stands alone.

We should note the significance of the scene in which Richard woos Anne over the body of her husband. This is not a record of an event; its tones should make us understand it to be the re-creation in Richard's imagination of the recollection of his wicked behaviour with Anne; he comments upon it with remembered glee. Later he has a similar scene with her mother, Queen Elizabeth, on the same subject, his conclusion being:

Relenting Foole, and shallow-changing Woman.
(4.4)

It has been pointed out that Richard's character does not develop; he is the same at the close of the play as at the beginning, as these two scenes demonstrate. Both the scenes have been objected to as unworthy of Shakespeare, but both are written with marked dramatic craftsmanship, and, understood as Richard's own version, their dramatic force is increased and their place in the play's action is clear.

What gives the play its interest and accounts for its hold upon audiences is the detachment of Richard in his wickedness. He watches himself, observes himself, looks on at himself in the mirror of his pride. When his detachment is allowed to be broken and he acts as

c*

himself, no longer the looker-on, the artist and the subject, he falls
to pieces as a dramatic figure, for the mirror, too, is broken. A drama
cannot be so written, a novel may be, not a play, because it is too
much to ask of an audience to participate in actual wickedness.

Written not only with poetic energy but with firm grasp upon
theatrical, apart from dramatic, essentials, this play has held the stage
while Marlowe's *Tamberlaine* has not.

THE LAMENTABLE TRAGEDY OF
TITUS ANDRONICUS (1592)

This strange play seems to be in the same category as *Richard III*,
and equally under the influence of *Tamberlaine*, for a powerful leading character that dominates the action is aimed at. Plays of murder,
cruelty, blood, and horror were meat and drink to Shakespeare's
theatre; yet Schlegel was right to recognize in this play beautiful
lines, bold images and features that betray Shakespeare's mind. Much
distaste has been expressed for it. Christopher Morley called it
"drivel" and there is something to be said for that point of view, but
if we accept the crudities and the prentice hand we shall find grandeur
and high poetry in it. The play starts full of action : there is so much
action, indeed, that it is easy to be confused as it proceeds to more
and more action, in which occur rape, mutilation, murder, and worse,
in the course of which Titus becomes "the wofull'st man that ever
lived in Rome". That the play is his, there can be no doubt. The
drama is, however, overwhelmed by violence, which does not belong
to reflection, so that the protagonist is not redeemed either by his
sufferings or the sufferings of others. The action is completed by
justice being done at the end through the confession of the villain,
but while the theatrical effect is satisfactory, the dramatic value is
negligible.

As I have pointed out, a marked weakness is that the leading
character is off the stage for too much of the action. Bradley said
that Shakespeare wrote this play before he had a dramatic conception;
but I think Shakespeare shows a very clear dramatic conception,
which gives the play great importance in the study of the development of his art. Hardin Craig in *An Interpretation of Shakespeare*
(1948) says "Titus Andronicus is theoretically—in intent and
structure—a very great tragedy. Practically it is not so". This is good

criticism, for the play fails because it is structurally weak, the protagonist not fulfilling his function. Titus is none the less designed as a true protagonist, a tragic hero, and, despite the ruthlessness and horror of his final action, awakens sympathy and understanding: consider for instance the respect with which he is treated after his death. The end he has in view is a noble one, the good of Rome,

> ... afterwards, to Order well the State,
> That like Events, may ne're it Ruinate.
>   (5.3)

The passions are so strong, however, that the noble end is dimmed. The play fails because the protagonist dies with his wrongs upon him, at the mercy of circumstances, without the sign of interior victory. The fact that the play closes with a just sentence upon the Moor, the villain of the piece, who defies death in the strongest possible language, indicates a mistaken tragic motive, and almost reduces the play to melodrama:

> I am no Baby I, that with base Prayers
> I should repent the Evils I have done.
> Ten thousand worse, than ever yet I did,
> Woulde I perform if I might have my will.
> If one good Deed in all my life I did,
> I do repent it from my very Soule.
>   (5.3)

Such excess of violence, moral and physical, as this play contains, makes it hard to witness, and causes it to be a drama in which it is barely possible to participate. For that reason, though popular in Elizabethan times, it has rarely been seen since, except when the hero has been presented as a mere character part. This is not so much because our stomachs are more delicate than our ancestors' as because the play is not sufficiently a play. Yet to call it melodrama, as H. B. Charlton does, is, I think, to do it injustice, for it is not written in the typical low-tragedy vein of melodrama, in which nothing is to be taken seriously; it has the style of serious drama. Consider its striking opening when Titus returns to Rome, after ten years of battles, bringing the bodies of his dead sons for burial, and when at the request of his surviving sons he gives in reparation the eldest son of the captured queen of the Goths to them for execution. This terrible scene is far above the level of melodrama and is to be visualized on a heroic scale. Titus is nominated as emperor, but refuses, and nominates instead the son of the late emperor to whom he gives the captive queen. His generosity is betrayed, for Lavinia, his daughter, whom he intends for the new emperor, who has asked for her as his empress, is carried off by the emperor's brother, supported by Titus's sons, one of whom in the fracas that occurs is stabbed by Titus. The new emperor then courts and weds his prisoner queen. Titus makes peace with his sons. The new emperor makes peace with Titus and his brother. This is the situation in the first act, which is a setting for high tragedy. The fact that some of us do not want to see it on the stage because of nightmarish agonies should not cause the play to be undervalued. Neither should Titus be treated as a mere mad-man. Certainly his sufferings make him mad, but he never loses his heroic poise. "When will this fearful slumber have an end," he says in contemplation of his vision of horrors. The hero's nobility and the play's poetical content make it bearable, and Aristotle cannot be quoted against it when he says:

> Those who employ spectacular means to create a sense not of the terrible, but only of the monstrous, are strangers to the purpose of Tragedy.

For there is nobility in spirit in this play, which for all its horrors, has a classical purity absent from *Richard III*.

THE TAMING OF THE SHREW (1593)

There is much controversy about this play being wholly Shakespeare's, and those who look for perfection introduce collaborators, which is not necessary. It is early work and faulty, but has always been popular, because it is easy for actors and audiences. All the same, it raises many questions and seems obviously imperfect. There are three plots: (1) that of the beggar who is treated as a lord and entertained with a play, but this plot ends when the play starts; (2) that of the shrewish daughter and the suitor who marries and tames her by force; (3) that of a second daughter who is wooed by suitors who enter her father's house in disguise. It is usual to treat the first plot as an induction to the play and it appears to have no other meaning: the expectations it arouses are not fulfilled. Its function seems to be to emphasize the unreality of the play itself, for a play set within a play is twice removed from Nature. Those who act it are seemingly intended to remain on the stage, though given no more to do. The main plot is the second, which contains Petruchio as the protagonist. He does not come on early, and is off the stage a great deal. He gets involved in the sub-plot, but it has nothing to do with him: these are the play's weaknesses. Petruchio's problem is to win Katherina, famed for her scolding. His is a comic figure:

> ... I have thrust myselfe into this maze,
> Happily to wive and thrive, as best I may ...
>
> (1.2)

He succeeds by sheer audacity and tireless energy. The entire play, with the exception of the Induction, is to be regarded as seen through Petruchio's eyes. The delight he has in subduing Katherina is infectious, and he invites the audience to share in it. The last speech by Katherina is clearly his; that a living woman ever spoke such words may be doubted, and what she says is what he would have her say:

> Thy husband is thy Lord, thy life, thy keeper,
> Thy head, thy soveraigne ...
> And craves no other tribute at thy hands,
> But love, fair lookes, and true obedience ...
> Then vale your stomackes, for it is no boote,
> And take your hands below your husband's foote:
> In token of which duty, if he please,
> My hand is readie, may it do him ease.
>
> (5.2)

The play is thus true drama; and to treat it as simple farce rather than farcical comedy is a mistake, for much is made of the characters, and we are intended to share in their predicaments as the protagonist presents them.

THE COMEDY OF ERRORS (1593)

This is Shakespeare's shortest play, over two thousand lines shorter than *Hamlet*, a version of a comedy by Plautus, and a very competently constructed piece. The commentators have not always thought well of it, and Quiller-Couch in particular seemed to have despised it because it went beyond Plautus by having two pairs of doubles, which he called an "impossible improbability". So indeed it is, regarding the play in the terms of life; but plays, as the critics strangely forget, are not life, and Shakespeare wrote under the magic of drama, even in so slight a thing as this. Quiller-Couch said in his disparagement (The New Shakespeare, 1922):

> . . . a play supposed to be acted by real persons exempt from magic must hold *some* claim of credence in its postulate, even though it call itself a farce.

But Shakespeare was not thinking of real persons, he did not suppose his play, or those who acted it, to be "exempt from magic", and the "credence" he sustained owed nothing to natural life. The play, truly, is an absurdity, but a genuine dramatic work.

Shakespeare introduces a protagonist, Aegeon, who is not in Plautus, thus converting the original into a true drama, which Plautus's was not. Aegeon appears only at the beginning and the end, in two scenes, and this infrequent presence is a serious weakness. An absent protagonist cannot but make a weak play, for he is unable properly to discharge his function. It is because he is absent so much that the play is made so absurd, for what a protagonist imagines is always exaggerated. Furthermore, he is unfortunate throughout, and much of the fun of the play is based upon this misfortune. Thus, while we sympathize with the protagonist, we can hardly admire him. This is an added weakness.

Quiller-Couch thought the play "fell to the ground", but he was honest enough to add that he had never seen it performed. It succeeds admirably on the stage, because it makes full use of stage mechanics, and only a practical stage worker could have written it.

It is worth noting that the play may show Shakespeare's early intimacy with the young men of the Inns of Court, a considerable population, important to the theatre, and much interested in London drama.

THE TWO GENTLEMEN OF VERONA (1593)

This charming work has never been a popular play because the protagonist is weak and the plot confused; there is much poetry and

the characters though slight are distinctive. So weak is the protagonist, however, that there is some doubt about who he is. There
are those who think he is Valentine, who is prominent at the play's
opening, but soon becomes a secondary character. Proteus, his friend,
might be the villain, for, though a romantic and attractive figure,
he plays false to his friend and to two young girls, which in a comic
piece is overmuch to tolerate, but he is undoubtedly the protagonist.
At the end he discards villainy:

> ...Oh heaven, were man
> But Constant, he were perfect; that one error
> Fills him with faults: makes him run through all th' sins;
> Inconstancy falls off, ere it begins.
>
> (5.4)

All the same his repentance is too late, and a protagonist who cannot
invite the audience to participate with him in his vision cannot
function well. Much fault is found with the text of the last act, but
the real trouble is the unsatisfactory nature of the dramatic action as
a whole.

The play concerns young men and was clearly intended for an
audience of young men. The characters are not flesh and blood but
creatures of fancy, and to judge them from the standpoint of real life
is to cause them to lose all the pleasure they can give.

The feature of the play is the large number of speeches in the nature
of soliloquy and thinking aloud. Wherever they occur they are part
of the play's action, whether the player comes forward or not. This
is not easy for actors taught to remain within the picture frame.
They occur in almost every other scene. Julia has the first in the
second scene of Act 1:

> And yet I would I had ore-look'd the Letter.
>
> (1.2)

she begins and ends the scene with a second:

> Nay, would I were so anger'd with the same.

In the next scene Proteus embarks upon a rhapsody, interrupted by
his father, so that he concludes the scene in another key:

> Thus have I shunn'd the fire, for feare of burning.
>
> (1.3)

In the third scene of Act 2 Launce comes in with his dog, with which he performs an amusing episode. The next scene concludes with Proteus saying:

> Even as one heate another heate expells,
> Or as one naile, by strength drives out another,
> So the remembrance of my former Love.
>
> (2.4)

The sixth scene is wholly taken up with Proteus's famous speech:

> To leave my Julia; shall I be forsworne?
> To love faire Silvia; shall I be forsworne?
> To wrong my friend, I shall be much forsworne.
>
> (2.6)

In the next Act, Valentine has a speech upon Silvia:

> And why not death, rather than living torment?
>
> (3.1)

Launce, the clownish servant, has a second solus performance. Then Proteus opens the serenade scene in which occurs the song "Who is Silvia", with:

> Already have I been false to Valentine,
> And now I must be as unjust to Thurio,
> Under the colour of commending him.
>
> (4.2)

Later in the same Act Launce has another performance with his dog, and in the last scene of the Act, Julia has a long reflective piece. And, to conclude, the last scene of the fifth Act is opened by Valentine with the speech:

> How use doth breed a habit in a man?

The treatment of these soliloquies is one of the play's practical problems, otherwise it is simple.

How far the conception of the play may be taken as Proteus's vision is open to doubt; but nothing is lost by recognizing it as such, and much gained, for the significance of the characters and action is increased, giving the play substance that it does not otherwise possess.

LOVE'S LABOUR'S LOST (1593)

This is another play of young men, intended to be played for young men, a play of poetic exuberance, exciting for its verbal excesses. Sober Hazlitt said, "If we were to part with any of the author's comedies, it should be this," but he would not willingly part with so charming a work. Undoubtedly it is one of the most pleasing of the plays, if one can be sufficiently young-hearted to enjoy the playing with words, able to laugh at the satire upon pedantry and to take pleasure in youthful figures in a garden. There is nothing but delight in it, and the play gains immensely in performance, showing unmistakable development in stage skill.

There is kinship with the later play A *Midsummer Night's Dream* and it is largely an entertainment for an occasion as was the later play. Yet there is drama in it, which the other does not possess, and a protagonist can clearly be distinguished in Berowne. He is the central figure of the young men, and what the royal party does, as well as the Princess and her ladies, all are seen through his eyes. The comic characters exist for "sport" and come within Berowne's vision only at a distance. This partly explains the play's weakness, of which most critics are conscious, for it dilutes the action, the comic episodes, excellent as they are, not appearing to belong to it, though they are brought in at the start and the characters are explicitly acknowledged by the King. Thus the play is defective on the grounds of what I consider to be Shakespeare's principle of drama.

The defect is structural, the play being a satire within a satire, the comic and romantic elements not sufficiently made one. It is, however, lavishly written, and its poetical content, gaiety, heart-easiness, and a heart-shaking close make it an admirable entertainment. Unfortunately it is too often played for plot rather than fancy, neither is its verse-form given sufficient attention, which does damage to its theatrical effectiveness. The discipline of the verse-form has to be respected for the play's values to be brought out.

Much critical attention has been paid to identifying the characters, which is made more difficult by the original 1593 play being rewritten for another performance, five years later, when the play was published, and (when it is possible) the merely comic characters had been changed for more topical reference. This must not detain us here, however, and has little relevance to the play's performance today, the satire being absorbed by the comedy.

The protagonist's problem is to reconcile his denial of love with love. He is caught out: in this lies the comedy. When Berowne says as the play opens:

> And though I have for barbarisme spoke more,
> Then for that Angel knowledge. . . .
>
> (1.1)

we are given the point of view from which we should receive it. The young men's cleverness, their "barbarism", is over-shot from the start. Berowne's speeches are a feature of the play and contain its theme. I need do no more than indicate this by quoting their opening lines:

> O, and I forsooth in love!
> I, that have been love's whip?
>
> (3.1)
>
> The King he is hunting the Deare,
> I am coursing myself . . .
>
> (4.3)
>
> Have at you then affection's men at armes. . . .
>
> (4.3)
>
> Thus poure the stars down plagues for perjury. . . .
>
> (5.2)

Though the play lends itself to detailed study, that is no part of my present task, which is only to point out that by recognizing Berowne's centrality a focus is provided for the action which otherwise it lacks.

THE SECOND PERIOD
(1594-1599)

Romeo and Juliet—Richard II—A Midsummer Night's Dream—King John—The Merchant of Venice—Henry IV, Part I—Henry IV, Part II—Much Ado About Nothing—Henry V—As You Like It.

H E R E are ten plays, written over a period of, say, five years, including some of Shakespeare's most important and most popular works, in which we can recognize the opening of a new phase of positive and creative dramatic energy, entirely different from what went before. Hitherto the plays have been a mere suggestion of what Shakespeare now began to write. These ten plays have weaknesses, undoubtedly, but there is increasing confidence until the dramatist can do exactly what he intends. Not one of these plays could have come from any other hand, and throughout the law of drama can be more and more clearly discerned until it is found in its purity. I remind the reader, once more, that I am considering the plays from a particular point of view and a single aspect making no attempt to deal with them otherwise.

THE TRAGEDY OF ROMEO AND JULIET (1594)

It is generally recognized that in *Romeo and Juliet* Shakespeare made a step forward in his art. Mr. H. B. Charlton puts it as :

. . . casting in fresh directions to find the universality, the momentousness, and above all the inevitability of all-compelling tragedy.

For my own part I should say that he was doing something more practical, endeavouring, in short, to establish a new dramatic standpoint. This standpoint was not the "inevitability" of the tragic outcome, but the controlling element in the dramatic action, which was found in constructing the play from the protagonist's point of view. There are hints of this in the earlier plays, but now for the first time the entire action is seen through the protagonist's eyes. It is true that there is "inevitability" of disaster, for the lovers are in the grip of necessity, but the drama is not in that alone. Not suffering or death, not fate, or misfortune, or wickedness, or a mistake constitutes the tragedy, though one or other or all may be there: the tragedy is the reconciliation in death, the ecstasy in union through disaster. If we were left with mere inevitability we should suffer pain at the lovers' terrible end, not be exalted by beauty. Why does the play move the spectator so deeply? Because the lovers' death and all that led up to it are presented in vision, and to present a sad tale as vision in the form of a dramatic action was, I suggest, Shakespeare's aim in this play, which I think he achieved.

We must admit that the play is not perfect as a whole, because Romeo, the protagonist, is indeed too much under the influence of necessity. He is not sufficiently central in the play's structure and is off the stage too much, thus weakening the dramatic backbone of the piece. That Pepys should have said, "a play of itself the worst that ever I heard, and the worst acted that I ever saw", (March 1, 1662), is no doubt explained by this fact, not disguised by Betterton, who played the part when Pepys saw it. Unless Romeo, strengthened by the actor's personality, is made central throughout by the actor's playing, the whole thing is handicapped. Sheer physical energy, which is required, is not alone sufficient; there has to be the brightest mental energy, a flaming imagination, with the actor in the right place in the play. To pay more attention to Juliet as though she could be made central does not strengthen the play but adds to its weakness.

Juliet as seen by Romeo is the divine girl, without a flaw. She never shows the slightest defect, but behaves perfectly as the ideal love of a young man should. Neither her parents nor anyone saw her in the light in which Romeo sees her in the play, she looks as lovers think their mistresses look, speaks so "silver-sweet" that the lover's heart melts; she is a vision bearing the tender bloom of virginity, no earthly girl at all. Every actress who attempts the part has a well-nigh impossible task. Only in dream not in real life are her lines credible:

> Come, gentle night; come loving, black-brow'd night,
> Give me my Romeo, and when he shall die,
> Take him and cut him out in little starres,

> And he will make the Face of heaven so fine
> That all the world will be in Love with night,
> And pay no worship to the Garish Sun.
>
> (3.2)

When she gets angry her anger has magic:

> What devil art thou,
> That dost torment me thus:
> This torture should be roar'd in dismall hell.

She was speaking to the Nurse rightly addressed as:

> Ancient damnation, O most wicked fiend!

Not alone Juliet, but the entire action of the play is elevated in Romeo's vision: the quarrel between the two families and the climax of his love. Romeo was not at the fracas with which the play starts, but imagines it, saying:

> Yet tell me not, for I have heard it all:
> Heere's much to do with hate, but more with love.
>
> (1.1)

Why "more with love", for his Rosaline, at that time his love, had nothing to do with this affair? Yet he goes on, as it were incoherently in relation to a situation that seemed to call for no such outburst:

> O brawling love, O loving hate:
> O anything of nothing, first created:
> O heavie lightnesse, serious vanity,
> Misshapen Chaos of wellseeing formes.

Is not Romeo as he views these quarrels seeing the end in the beginning? The tragedy thus appears at the play's opening, for at the opening the end in the sense of the dramatic vision had already been reached.

Romeo imagines, too, the brief Capulet scene in which Paris is urged to woo Juliet; then the letter about Capulet's supper, to which he had decided to go for Rosaline's sake:

> One fairer than my love: the all-seeing Sun
> Nere saw her match, since first the world begun.
>
> (1.2)

This is Rosaline, not Juliet, but we do not distinguish her at the supper. Before it, there is a scene in which the nurse displays her devilish quality and there is women's talk about Juliet's proposed marriage. Then Romeo appears again with his friends, as masquers, on the way to the supper, followed by the supper and the fatal meeting. Rosaline is forgotten. At the end of the act Juliet's words are Romeo's thoughts, for she is wholly Romeo's. Then, after a brief speech from the Chorus, who makes his only appearance, not being needed again, Romeo sees Juliet on the balcony. This is such a scene as lovers dream of:

> It is my Lady, O it is my Love, O that she knew she were. . . .
>
> (2.2)

When it ends, after a thousand good nights, Romeo meets the Friar to tell him

> . . . my hearts deare Love is set,
> On the faire daughter of rich Capulet;
> As mine on hers, so hers is set on mine,
> And all combin'd, save what thou must combine
> By holy marriage.
>
> (2.3)

After the marriage in the Friar's cell there is a brief sweet meeting between them, followed by the terrible scene in which Mercutio is killed by Tybalt and Tybalt by Romeo, resulting in the Prince declaring exile on Romeo. This fight was Romeo's mistake, the turning point in the dramatic action. Then after their night together the lovers part to meet again in the tomb. The interval is as Romeo sees it in imagination, painful, desperate and exaggerated. Finally the fatal close, ecstatic, exciting in the highest degree, with Romeo's wonderful speech over Juliet, and Juliet's words when she awakens:

> O happy Dagger . . .
>
> (5.3)

The conclusion brings a peaceful end to the family strife:

> See what a scourge is laide upon your hate,
> That Heaven finds meanes to kill your joyes with Love.

It is sad, but joyful; full of pain, but lighted with beauty; there is punishment, but redemption too; there is chance, but we feel the hand of Providence. These lovers will remain perfect for ever.

I have thus briefly gone through the action to show how everything is related to Romeo, for it is in his view of these happenings that he invites the audience to participate.

As I have pointed out, the play suffers from the slightness of the protagonist and in particular his helplessness. The tragedy is precipitated by his hasty attack upon Tybalt after the latter had killed Mercutio, but what else could the young hero have done? Romeo is hemmed in by necessity and his free will has little scope. He walks through the play wholly in dream. This has always been regarded as a dramatic weakness, causing critics to wish that more had been made of Mercutio; but that character is secondary to the action and has soon to be disposed of. Shakespeare was uncertain about Mercutio, said Granville Barker, without justification, for his place was to provide the occasion for the turning point. Full of colour and rhetoric the character is decoration apart from its essential technical function.

Another point is that the tragedy is outward; the hero appears to have no soul: he seems not to have grown up. He is a child in love, never adult and responsible. Except for sweetness the play is strangely empty, though it touches the heart, for these two young things, thrown together, torn asunder, offering their lives as fulfilment, are pitiful. "Never was a story of more woe."

I conclude with a note on the factor of time. The action of the play up to the supposed death of Juliet appears to take three days and nights. The opening occurs on one day; on the same night are the supper and first balcony scene; on the second day the marriage, at night the second balcony scene; the third day the announcement of the marriage with Paris, and at night Juliet's supposed death. Looking at these events from a story-teller's point of view it is obvious that some weeks must have passed between the meeting and the secret marriage, then some months before Tybalt is slain and Romeo exiled, and the whole summer has gone by before the completion of the marriage arrangements with Paris. This has the progress of events in actuality, but the play is not a repetition of what took place, there is no concern with time and even to think of three days is unnecessary. The play is vision, with the experience as it exists in Romeo's mind in which time has no meaning. All attempts to work out the time-sequence are bound to fail, because the play has none; it is beyond time. Only what Berdyaev called "existential time" applies; he explained the term to mean:

> Existential time may best be symbolized . . . by the point . . . the still point of the turning world.

Hitherto, the question of the ambiguities of time in many of the plays has been unanswerable. It has been excused by bad craftsmanship, or the handicaps of the Elizabethan stage, or sheer carelessness. No such explanations, I suggest, need to be considered. In the vision that constitutes drama there is no time, only timelessness, the eternal Now.

Time is what the dramatist choses to make it, and it is the same with place. As time is simultaneous, so all places are one place. Place is immaterial. Yes, there was place, but the mind of the protagonist moves from place to place, merging place with place, for in vision place has no more reality than time. The action of the plays occurs in an imitation of time and space because drama is limited by concreteness, so that to ignore time and space is not possible; but they become symbols, not repetitions of actual life and natural effects are out of place. Though day and night can be recognized, also the passage of years, there is no tying down to the processes of life. The characters and situations have escaped from actuality and become real in vision. No problems of time and place are involved in the attempt to understand any of the plays. Those who are bothered by them are troubling themselves unnecessarily, for except on the stage, where such problems may be practically encountered, they are the invention of those who attempt to bring works of imagination down to earth.

Dramatic unity in Shakespeare does not lie in time and place any more than in the rationality of the plot, or the consistency of the characters. The principle of unity is in the coherent vision of the protagonist.

THE LIFE AND DEATH OF RICHARD II (1595)

In this play Shakespeare returned to history for a tragic theme, for the sake of a "star in the sky", as Coleridge said. The hero has always been a favourite with actors and audiences. He is glamorous, excites admiration and pity, and presents a picture of all-too-human greatness cast down and destroyed, which never fails to appeal. The action is that of an unstable man in a position demanding stability of character, and is developed as Richard sees it: his friends, his enemies, and his defeat and abdication are as he presents them in imagination. So understood, the tragic effect of the play is greatly heightened, as compared with its effect as history or as an essay in politics. It is sweet and tender, and profoundly moving as an experience that all can share or enter into.

In fact, this king is by no means wholly admirable, for he appears to be homosexual, causing him to be unbalanced and wayward, with the result that he wastes his kingdom, and his behaviour calls for rebellion. This grave fault is not disguised in the play, but is set in the light of the king's own eyes not as others saw it. Looked at objectively, another story could be told, but we are invited to view it as does the hero himself. Who can suppose that the action is not presented from Richard's point of view, for from the opening of the play by Richard himself to its close with Bolingbroke's words:

> Ile make a voyage to the Holy-land,
> To wash this blood off from my guilty hand.
>
> (5.5)

the play contains nothing but what is present to Richard's mind? Indeed, in his final soliloquy, Richard declares:

> My Braine, Ile prove the Female to my Soule,
> My Soule, the Father: and these two beget
> A generation of still breeding Thoughts:
> And these same Thoughts, people this Little World
> In humors like the people of this world.
>
> (5.4)

Who can doubt that all that is said and done beats into music with meaning for him?

What John of Gaunt says in Richard's absence, including his famous speech of prophecy, is Richard in meditation, not as his uncle spoke, who was not in fact very old, though old to Richard, neither was he the noble character Richard chooses to see in him. Gaunt's death-episode is Richard's judgement on himself, otherwise it is difficult to explain; for why give Gaunt the first good speech in the play, unless the thoughts are Richard's? Bolingbroke, the King's contemporary, and his ambitious and unscrupulous enemy, has the will-power, the self-control and pushing energy that Richard lacks, and appears in an uncompromising light, yet he is presented without hatred in Richard's comprehending vision.

This tolerating insight is never to be overlooked in the study of the play, and unless kept in mind in reading and performance the play's profound dramatic value cannot be brought out. Consider what Richard says immediately after Bolingbroke's banishment, which can hardly have been the words used at the time:

> Ourselve, and Bushy : heere Bagot and Greene
> Observ'd his Courtship to the common people :
> How he did seeme to dive into their hearts,
> With humble, and familiar courtesie
> What reverence he did throw away on slaves;
> Wooing poor Craftsmen with the craft of smiles,
> And patient underbearing of his Fortune,
> As 'twer to banish their affects with him . . .
> As were our England in reversion his,
> And he our subjects' next degree in hope.
>
> (1.4)

Green discounts these remarks; in fact, of course, they were never uttered, or they would have had to be taken seriously and the course of events might have changed. How these words should be said by the actor needs much thought, for to take them naturally is to make nonsense of the play.

The turning point in the dramatic action is Richard's folly in going off to Ireland, leaving his kingdom in the hands of his father's uncle, York. When Richard returns to England his lyric outburst cannot be explained on naturalistic grounds at a moment when physical action was demanded, only on the grounds of dramatic action of the nature I have indicated.

Richard offers no excuses for his tragedy. He is self-propelled to his fall. He was done double wrong by flatterers, even the deadly flattery of Bolingbroke. There is no emphasis upon the political ambitions of his enemies.

He is not concerned to set himself in a favourable light, for dead redeemed souls do not need justification. Note how callous he sees himself to have been when he hears of Gaunt's sickness:

> Now put it (heaven) in his Physician's minde,
> To helpe him to his grave immediately :
> The lining of his coffers shall make Coates

To deck our soldiers for these Irish warres.
Come, Gentlemen, let's all go visit him;
Pray heaven we may make haste, and come too late.

(1.4)

No doubt he had said no such thing, but that was what he thought in retrospect, remembering Gaunt with sympathy and honour, as the next scene shows. Gaunt is flattered and made memorable, while Richard is abominable. In fact Richard is set on his pathway of destruction, for the events that follow are its direct consequence. Such is the candour of truth.

Richard does not appear again in the play until the second scene of the third act. In the interval we get insight into the national dissatisfaction, and pictures of the Queen's despair, the revolt against Richard in favour of Bolingbroke, the latter's return and grasp for power, and his execution of Richard's favourites. This is not mere narrative but, as it were, Richard's building up of the situation. Then Richard faces his nakedness, covered only in the divine annointment of his office:

> Not all the Water in the rough rude Sea
> Can wash the Balme from an annoynted King;
> The breath of worldly men cannot depose
> The Deputie elected by the Lord.

(3.2)

He is debased, loses the name of king, and looks into the opening grave. These marvellous scenes are unexcelled, even in Shakespeare, except by the scene that follows in the fourth act, in which Richard is made to resign the crown, formally, and to condemn himself:

> Oh, that I were a Mockerie, King of Snow,
> Standing before the Sunne of Bolingbroke,
> To melt myselfe away in Water-drops.

(4.1)

After that there is only acceptance of his fate and resignation of soul.

Marlowe's *Edward II* produced in 1592, three years earlier, has the same theme, and though a most interesting work lacks the substance, quality and dramatic energy of Shakespeare's play, which is clearly seen in a comparison of the two abdication scenes. Marlowe's is a true drama, however, being presented from the King's point of view. The two plays should be read together, when it will be perceived that the sublimity of thought that characterizes Shakespeare's play is accompanied by a firmer grasp upon the law of drama than is shown by Marlowe, the outcome of Shakespeare's greater playwriting experience.

A MIDSUMMER NIGHT'S DREAM (1595)

Everyone is agreed that this play was written to entertain the guests at a wedding. Thus it is to be regarded as a marriage entertainment, which explains why it is not a drama in the strict sense, lacking the essential element of a protagonist. For who could be the protagonist here? No one but Theseus; but the Duke of Athens though he opens the play and ends it does not have even a comic problem, and does not project himself into the action of the play. He is not really concerned with the distress of Egeus over his daughter, or with the tangles of the lovers, or with the antics of the artisans of the city, much less with the conflict in fairy-land, only with "our nuptiall houre", and with the merriment that should accompany it. Though he backs up parental authority in Egeus, he does so as a matter of mere duty. So severe is he with the girl who will not obey her father and so "over-full of self-affairs" that he warns her to fit her fancies to her father's will . . .

> Or else the Law of Athens yields you up . . .
> To death, or to a vow of single life.
>
> (1.1)

Yet he has no other thought for himself and in the end for all the lovers than . . .

> Sweet friends to bed.
>
> (5.1)

Though written for rhetorical delivery the poetry does not appear to aim at dramatic creation. I think Bottom gives the key to the play when he says:

> I have had a most rare vision. I had a dreame, past the wit of man, to say, what dreame it was. Man is but an Asse, if he goe about to expound this dreame . . . The eye of man hath not heard, the eare of man hath not seen, man's hand is not able to taste, his tongue to conceive, nor his heart to report, what my dreame was. I will get Peter Quince to write a ballet of this dreame, It shall be called Bottomes Dreame, because it hath no bottome. . . .   (4.1)

That should be conclusive, and we should proceed no further. To see more in the play than Shakespeare is willing to show is to waste time. The speech of Theseus with which the last act opens explains the right attitude towards the play:

> I never may beleeve
> These anticke fables, nor these Fairy toyes,
> Lovers and mad men have such seething braines,
> Such shaping plantasies, that apprehend more
> Than coole reason ever comprehends.
>
> (5.1)

A feature is the way in which the different interests of the Court, the lovers, the artisans and the fairies are interwoven to make a whole. It is a masterly piece of theatrical construction.

Hazlitt thought that the play "when acted, is converted from a delightful fiction into a dull pantomime. All that is finest in the play is lost. . . ." What is finest is the poetry, which calls for a stage that enables the actors to speak it rightly; but poetry apart, the work has theatricality, which also needs the right stage to suit it. Usually it becomes mere spectacle and is handed over to scene designer and comedians. That Shakespeare did not disdain entertainment as such, we may be sure, and here he showed what he could make of it when he chose, devoting to it some of his finest poetry and comic invention. The importance of the play in relation to Shakespeare the dramatist is that it is an example of a work in which, apparently quite deliberately, the law of drama is ignored.

THE LIFE AND DEATH OF KING JOHN (1596)

There is some doubt as to the relation between this play and a supposed earlier work, and there are some who think the earlier work also to have been Shakespeare's. Possibly the influence of the early work may be detected in the confused action, and the uncertainty about who is the protagonist. He should be King John, but it is impossible to accept that function for the king, for his problem, which is how to keep his crown, raises questions that are by no means sympathetic to him. With the king as protagonist the play would be tragedy of an unpleasing kind. Therefore the Bastard, Faulcon-bridge, must be accepted as the leading character, for he is held up for admiration, is brave and patriotic, and his strength is contrasted with the weakness of the king. Says Mr. H. B. Charlton of the play in his *Shakespearean Tragedy* (1948):

> . . . its course as it runs is fashioned by Falconbridge. The plot is England's well-being; and as far as that well-being is ostensibly promoted in the play, it is the direct result of Falconbridge's presence. Moreover it is incontestibly the visible result of Falconbridge's character, his personality and his outlook on life.

This can be agreed, but I cannot agree with Mr. Charlton when he says on the same page that "The hero of the play is England", for an abstraction, or a non-personal thing, cannot be a dramatic hero. Irony is a dangerous method and the extremely ironical character of the protagonist makes the play unsatisfactory to naturalistically minded actors and causes it to be rarely performed. In truth it is a fine play with splendidly theatrical scenes, and strong if rather confused drama, touching and human and containing much poetry.

John is a weak king, who cannot keep his throne, though he is ready to stick at nothing in attempting to do so. The turning point of the plot is the murder of the boy prince, Arthur, who by right should be on the throne: after that murder we feel that John deserves to be poisoned. John's weakness is not merely one of character, it also lies in his unsure title to the throne; but it is nothing but defect of character, the sheer inability to be honest, that brings him to his ghastly end:

> Poison'd, ill fare : dead, forsooke, cast off,
> And none of you will bid the winter come
> To thrust his icie fingers in my maw;
> Nor let my kingdome's Rivers take their course
> Through my burn'd bosome : nor intreat the North
> To make his bleake windes kiss my parched lips,
> And comfort me with cold. I do not aske you much,
> I begge cold comfort : and you are so straight
> And so ingratefull, you deny me that.
>
> (5.7)

There is no sympathy for him, and when he dies, Faulconbridge says

> Now, now you Starres, that move in your right spheres,
> Where be your powers?

And turning to the lords about the body of the King, he goes on

> Shew now your mended faiths,
> And instantly returne with me againe
> To push destruction, and perpetual shame
> Out of the weak doore of our fainting Land.
>
> (5.7)

This Faulconbridge, earlier in the play, declaring that he perceived how "tickling commoditie", or one's own interests, is what influences men in the world, says in a soliloquy, direct to the audience, what must be intended to be bitter irony:

> Since Kings breake faith upon commoditie,
> Gaine be my Lord, for I will worship thee.
>
> (1.2)

To understand this and other expressions as an exposition of the hero's own state of mind is a serious error, for were it the truth it could not be reconciled with his patriotism, which is unquestioned, so that the character would become split. Yet when the action of the play, the king and all the characters, are seen through Faulconbridge's eyes, and the entire play as his statement or vision of events, the play becomes coherent and may be admitted to be perhaps the greatest of the political plays, the most ruthless, involving the largest number of men, all false, all serving commodity—except the Bastard. None the less, the protagonist is not handled with the centrality drama requires, which I think accounts for its relative weakness.

THE MERCHANT OF VENICE (1596)

Here we come to one of the most popular and altogether pleasing of the plays, a work of admitted imagination uncloyed by fact, but puzzling to commentators and actors because the largest and most important character is not the protagonist. So deeply is this felt that it is thought to be "a carelessly constructed and incredible play". The distinguished Quiller-Couch applied the words "bad workman-ship" to it. From the point of view of life in Venice or London, the incredibility is true, but to speak of bad workmanship is true only if the position of the protagonist is meant.

Antonio, the merchant of Venice, unmistakably the protagonist,

is given nothing like the dimensions of Shylock, the villain. Shakespeare does not allow him a house or servants. This is a terrible
handicap upon those who treat the play naturalistically, attempting
to make the plot credible, because they do not know what to do with
Antonio, so that the part is usually given to an inferior actor who
wanders lost throughout the play. This was not intended by the
dramatist, as study of the play reveals, and comes from mis-under-
standing the play as a record of events, not seeing that it is a fairy
tale, its action belonging to an imaginary world to which its
characters belong. When Antonio and Shylock are together (1.3) the
stage is Antonio's not Shylock's. Antonio must not be pushed to the
side while Shylock displays himself master of the situation. He is
not, in fact, master of the situation, for Antonio is employing him.
When they meet again in 3.3, their positions are reversed, for Antonio
is in charge of a gaoler, and at Shylock's mercy, but none the less
he must not be obscured by the monstrous figure, for the stage is
still his. At the trial, he is called forward by the Duke. This means
that the actor playing Antonio must be conscious throughout of his
status. He is not on the stage merely to fulfil the needs of the plot.
Though over-shadowed by the greater character, he must stand and
move on the stage as its owner. All that takes place is to be judged
from the point of view of imagination, with Antonio central, the
play his, he being responsible directly or indirectly for the action,
all of which is related to him.

Antonio's problem is how to get out of his rash bond to the Jew.
The action of the play is concerned with this problem and presents
a clash between those attached to real and to illusionary wealth. The
trial scene before the Duke is the climax of the plot, but the casket
scene is the centre of the play's inner action, for that scene is intended
to provide a test of worth. Is real worth in the Jew's values—money,
business acuteness and trickery—or is it in friendship, loyalty, and
the poetry of life? That is the inner question the play raises.
Antonio's action in helping his friend as he did was rash, even foolish,
certainly odd behaviour in an experienced merchant! Its rightness
or sense, however, is taken for granted as the sort of thing friend
will do for friend, the worth of friendship being in such odd actions,
so that this foolish action provides the dramatic motive for the
comedy.

Antonio speaks first in the play. He has become unusually serious,
he says, without knowing why. He is not intended to be spiritless

or depressed, for which there was no reason. If from this point we press too closely into the rationality of the plot we shall wonder how it happened that Antonio needed to be bound to the Jew, and being bound was unable to meet his obligation, for the opening makes clear that he had ample resources:

> My ventures are not in one bottome trusted,
> Nor to one place: nor is my whole estate
> Upon the fortune of this present yeare.
>
> (1.1)

Having said this, why should he declare himself to be in a difficulty over raising money for Bassanio's pressing needs? These questions, however, do not need to be followed, for the drama does not invite us to consider the rationality of life, but to enter into a situation created by generosity. A rich and generous merchant puts himself, for the sake of his friend, into peril: all flows from that. The Jew, monster that he is, as all usurers were to Shakespeare's audience, is incidental. So, indeed, are Portia and her suitors, and among them the aforementioned friend. The incidental elements, however, make the play's relish, for the lovely, rich, and generous Portia, lucky in satisfying her desires, witty, daring, learned, is a marvellous character . . .

> . . . a Lady richly left,
> And she is faire, and fairer than that word,
> of wondrous virtues.
>
> (1.1)

All is wondrous that belongs to Portia, for Antonio sees her only in imagination until the end. And Shylock is a remarkable creation, one of the outstanding characters in the whole of drama.

An apparent difficulty is the joining of the play's two themes, Antonio's bond to the Jew, and the marriage of Portia, but the difficulty is mainly the familiar one arising from the endeavour to establish time and place. The play's scene is Venice, and the conflict occurs there; Portia lives at Belmont. Clearly the dramatist's intention is to contrast remote, ideal, and love-set Belmont, with the actualities of money-making Venice, as well as to contrast the honest business man, Antonio, with the unscrupulous money lender, Shylock. The play is crowded with theatricality as well as with dramatic action: the bond, the test of the caskets, the flight of Jessica, the loss of the

D

merchant's fortunes, the trial, the incident of the rings, and the sweetness of music and night.

The episodes in Belmont where Antonio does not appear are exquisite, for they are as he imagines them, and possess the remoteness and perfection of pure vision. Not a touch of the crudity of natural life falls upon them. The casket episode, in itself absurd, is a lovely fairy tale, and to treat it as real life is nonsense. Portia, herself, is a heroine without a speck upon her, observed with the eyes of one who wishes her well, for has not Antonio risked his all for the sake of her lover's happiness? Antonio does not see her until the trial, when he thinks he is looking on someone else. What Bassanio sees does not matter, nor Gratiano either, though that they should fail to recognize their loves is possible only in fairy tale. Bassanio, the young lover, for whose sake Antonio enters into the bond, is nothing of a character though he has splendid lines, yet the part counts in the dramatic action, because of Antonio's devotion to him:

> The world is still deceiv'd with ornament . . .

is what he says himself.

The dream-like nature of the play is displayed to the full, its rapture only seemingly disturbed by pretended quarrels in the last scene:

> The moone shines bright. In such a night as this
> When the sweete winde did gently kisse the trees,
> And they did make no noise . . .
> In such a night . . .
>
> (5.1)

The words six times repeated, "In such a night", spread calm after the storm of the Jew's defeat. No mention is made of him, for he was vanished from a peaceful world. Antonio is there, of course, his first appearance at Belmont,

> Sweete Ladie, you have given me life and living . . .

In the scene's dream-likeness lies the reminiscence, the re-living, the vision in Antonio's mind and makes the comedy: the entrance of the mind of the audience into Antonio's mind, its sympathy and understanding, should be complete.

THE FIRST PART OF KING HENRY THE FOURTH (1597)

This is one of the plays in which the protagonist is not indicated in the title. Who he is has been disputed. It cannot be Henry the Fourth, for he says as much in the opening:

> So shaken as we are, so wan with care.
>
> (1.1)

The King is a dying man; the brave Bolingbroke of *Richard II*, after four years on the stolen throne, is full of trouble in the state and full of sickness in himself. There are those who hesitate about Hotspur, who is admired by the King and held up for the admiration of all; but he turns out to be a rebel, is slain, and rightly dismissed:

> Ill-weav'd Ambition, how much art thou shrunk.
>
> (5.4)

Others plump for Falstaff, as did Quiller-Couch,

> Falstaff is no sooner introduced than he takes charge and establishes himself as the real hero of the play.

This seems sheer perversity, equal to Quiller-Couch's preference for Falstaff over the Prince, in which he follows Hazlitt, as "the better man of the two". After this error, the same critic is led to a discovery:

> It has set up a permanent artistic principle in the treatment of history by fiction; the principle that, in drama or novel of this kind, your best protagonists, and the minor characters you can best treat with liveliness as with philosophy, are not those concerning whose sayings and doings you are circumscribed by known fact and documentary evidence, but rather some invented men or women—pawns in the game—upon whose actions and destinies you can make the great events play at will.

This remarkable sentence calls for a little attention, for although the writer later on claims the authority of Aristotle, "who first laid hold of the secret", there is no substance in Quiller-Couch's attempt to use his new artistic principle in support of his claim for Falstaff. A protagonist is always invented, even though a person bearing the name once existed; for dramatic invention is the dramatist's business. Unless this be accepted, dramatist and spectators are lost, and playwrights would be condemned, as honest men, to relating versions of history that could be sworn to. Then the stage would be silenced, for history, too, is a form of art, and the newspaper itself a "story", and both would supplant the drama.

To suppose that Falstaff could be the protagonist is to be indifferent to the true function of a protagonist, who is not merely a large, or likeable, or energetic character: he is the one who invites the spectators to listen and to participate and through whose eyes the whole affair is unfolded. Is this play seen through Falstaff's eyes, and is its action a poetic re-creation in his mind? The question has only to be asked to be seen to be absurd.

The protagonist is Prince Hal, Shakespeare's darling, though

> Ryot and Dishonour staine the brow
> Of my young Harry.
>
> (1.1)

He is the play's hero, riotous and shameful in behaviour, but true to his father and not altogether forgetful of his princely duty. Quiller-Couch, whom I may be forgiven for quoting once more, because of his critical eminence, could not endure the Prince's soliloquy, which closes the first Falstaff scene: "The most damnable piece of workmanship to be found in any of his plays," he says, and goes on,

> This, if we accept it, poisons what follows, poisons the madcap Prince in our imagination for good and all.

And the critic does his best to suppose that Burbage or some other impudent actor induced the glorious Shakespeare to put in the words. But they must be accepted as authentic Shakespeare, and only excess of sentimentality over Falstaff and belief in the play being as near as possible to natural life could have led to any dislike of the speech. Let us look at it. Says the Prince, Falstaff and Poins having left:

> I know you all, and will a while uphold
> The unyoak'd humour of your idlenesse;
> Yet herein will I imitate the Sunne,
> Who doth permit the base contagious cloudes
> To smother up his Beauty from the world,
> That when he please again to be himselfe,
> Being wanted, he may be more wondered at,
> By breaking through the foule and ugly mists
> Of vapours, that did seem to strangle him.
> If all the years were playing holidaies,
> To sport, would be as tedious as to worke;
> But when they seldome come, they wisht-for come,

And nothing pleaseth but rare accidents.
So when this loose behaviour I throw off,
And pay the debt I never promised;
By how much better than my word I am,
By so much shall I falsifie men's hopes,
And like bright Mettall on a sullen ground :
My reformation glittering o're my fault,
Shall show more goodly, and attract more eyes,
Then that which hath no foyle to set it off.
Ile so offend, to make offence a skill,
Redeeming time, when men thinke least I will.

(1.2)

Accepting Quiller-Couch's standpoint that the play should have the rationality of Nature, and the morality of Cambridge, these are perhaps shocking words; but rejecting that standpoint utterly, as we do, and accepting the play as an imaginary work in which Prince Hal as protagonist invites the audience to participate with him in a vision of events, the words are self-explanatory and cause no mental trouble, only delight. This is not the Hal who had just left Falstaff who is speaking but another Hal who once we understand what the dramatist is doing brings us no pangs.

Falstaff is, of course, a marvel, there is no character to equal him in the entire range of drama. He is everything that is objectionable, including his physical appearance, but there is no character more loved. He is presented with the utmost candour; yet because his mere humanity is seen clearly without disguise of any kind we take him to our hearts. He is the quintessence of the natural man elevated to the sphere of imagination, so that he is larger than life, and it is fittingly said of him :

What a devil hast thou to do with the time of the day?

His words rumble up from the cavernous depths of the enormous stomach, embellished by nimble wit and horse sense as the juicy tones proceed through the well-oiled throat. He fills the play and the stage, and when he appears there are no eyes for anyone else, not even for Hal. Yet let us note that when he appears Hal is never far away. His greatness is due to the place he holds in Hal's vision.

The same is to be said of Hotspur, who is so generous, so high-spirited, so free from the politicians' guile : that is how the Prince saw him : the requiem is a wholehearted and honest tribute to an admired foe, who should have been a friend. To take a low view of

Hal is to take a superficial view. When Hotspur reads the letter (2.3) we should hear Hal speaking.

It cannot be denied that it is a weakness in the play for Hal to be so little with the King that the affairs of state hardly exist in his presence. It gives him an inferior place. Yet that, no doubt, was what was intended by the dramatist, and we must accept the convention that what the Prince does not in fact see he none the less clearly imagines. Hal is re-established at the end in the King's favour. The recognition of the law of drama raises no problems in this play but solves them.

THE SECOND PART OF KING HENRY THE FOURTH (1596)

A prologue and epilogue are notable, the first spoken by a character called Rumour, the second by an unspecified character, who claims to be a dancer. In this play, Prince Hal, still the protagonist, increases in importance until he becomes King. Falstaff, larger than ever, displays himself at his worst and best and is finally discarded. The problem of the play to the critics is how could Hal on becoming king cast off Falstaff? "Harry," says Quiller-Couch bitterly, "wronged Falstaff and killed his heart". We are to understand that for such behaviour this reformed rake cannot be forgiven. It is difficult to have patience with such nonsense; only by misunderstanding what Shakespeare was doing could it be entertained.

In this second part the Prince has to carry out what he had announced about himself at the beginning of the first part, to throw off his "loose behaviour". He has a remarkable scene with his dying father, when the King being unconscious the Prince takes the crown and places it upon his own head. When the unhappy King dies, the Prince becomes a different man. He says of the man he was:

> I have long dream'd of such a kinde of man . . .
> But being awake, I do despise my dreame.

(5.5)

Bradley considered that in Falstaff Shakespeare "overshot his mark", which explains why Falstaff's rejection is so hard to accept. The poet had created "a man of genius" too great for the play, thought the critic, and his necessary dismissal was too much even for Shakespeare to make tolerable. This, too, seems to me to be nonsense. All is dream: and though much takes place without the presence of the protagonist, including almost all the Falstaff scenes, they too are part of the dream and are to be considered as within the range of the Prince's vision.

It is an admirable play.

MUCH ADO ABOUT NOTHING (1598)

There are changes to be noted in Shakespeare's art. Here comedy is raised to a level that ranks it with the tragedies, the new element being the dramatist's treatment of women. For the first time he creates a woman character who is only just short of being a protagonist. Beatrice is one of Shakespeare's greatest characters, yet not the leading character, though perhaps she should have been. Benedick is the protagonist, and the play is his. It might have been entitled the "Humanising of Benedick", for that is its theme.

The title of this play may be satirical, for the "nothing" is how the events of the plot appear to the young men of fashion who are satirized. A young girl is slandered and denounced, and supposed to be dead as a consequence, which is "nothing" to young rich men of the world. The Prince, his friends, Claudio and Benedick, and his brother Don John, are Renaissance men, clever, witty, idle, except for sport and soldiering, hard and callous, who have little human feeling: such young men were no doubt familiar to Shakespeare. The "renowned Claudio" fancies Hero when he sees her for the first time, and quickly arranges to marry her; but being told a trumped-up story of unfaithfulness, as quickly denounces her before the marriage without attempting to examine the story. There is no need to probe into this too closely, because we are intended to accept it on the dramatist's word, but it puts the young men in a poor light, as every critic agrees.

Benedick, however, has fallen in love with Beatrice, and she with him, aided by some innocent trickery in which the other characters share; and the heights of comedy are reached when, at the close of the broken marriage scene, Benedick and Beatrice are left alone, pretences are thrown aside and callousness is torn from him by the passionate devotion of Beatrice to her traduced friend, and faced with reality he becomes a man. The "kill Claudio" scene, one of the most moving, skilful, and amazing scenes in Shakespeare, is very difficult for the actors, and the turning point of the play.

The entire play is to be understood from Benedick's point of view. His problem is his love for Beatrice, which has taken him by surprise:

> I did never thinke to marry, I must not seeme proud, happy are they that heare their detractions, and can put them to mending . . . the world must be peopled. When I said I would die a batchelor, I did not think I should live till I were married.   (2.3)

She, too, is taken by surprise:

> What fire is in mine eares? Can this be true?
>   (3.1)

And when they are at last alone, after the shock of the denouncement of the bride, their joint confession ravishes the heart, Benedick beginning:

> I doe love nothing in the world so well as you, is not that strange?

> As strange as the thing I know not, it were as possible for me to say, I loved nothing so well as you, but believe me not, and yet I lie not, I confesse nothing, nor I deny nothing. I am sorry for my cousin . . .

> I protest I love thee.

> Why then God forgive me.

> What offence sweet Beatrice?

> You have stayed me in a happy houre, I was about to protest I loved you.

> And doe it with all thy heart.

> I love you with so much of my heart, that none is left to protest.

> Come, bid me do anything for thee.

> Kill Claudio.

> Ha, not for the wide world.   (4.1)

This shattering demand was the last thing Benedick expected. After it, there are no more pretences: he must do as she says. Shakespeare never wrote a more moving scene. As the play proceeds there is increasing tension, until Claudio, too, has his heart touched by the facts coming to light, after which there is reconciliation.

How skilfully the play is constructed! There was a moment when the bride's father had the opportunity thrust upon him of knowing the truth before the event and so preventing the unhappiness to his daughter, but he brushed it aside. The grotesque comic character, Dogberry, looms out of the mass of common men, an individual, supremely stupid, the essence of ridiculous self-centredness. As Benedick never encounters him, he exists only in vision, and is therefore more absurd than life. No one seeing the Dogberry scenes supposes thy are a simple record of fact. They are much more and have a part in the process of making a man of Benedick, which is the vision contained in the play.

The end is on the highest note of assurance in the terms of comedy:

> Ile tell thee what Prince: a College of wise-crakers cannot flout mee out of my humour, dust thou think I care for a Satyre or an Epigram? no, if a man will be beaten with braines, he shall weare nothing handsome about him. . . .   (5.4)

No comedy surpasses this in the entire range of drama.

THE LIFE OF HENRY THE FIFTH (1599)

Whether Shakespeare had in mind in this play the epic picture of England that Dr. W. M. W. Tillyard and others suppose is to me a matter of grave doubt, for I do not think that except in a secondary sense Shakespeare was concerned with history. All the same it is legitimate to get out of the plays as much as one can; but understanding of them is contained, I think, essentially in the dramatic theme, and to go beyond it is to be in danger of losing the play's meaning, which is concerned with the immediate moment and the state of mind of the audience.

In this play there is a popular king whose problem is to secure the national interest and to make safe his throne in that interest. It is the theme of patriotism, a familiar and urgent theme to the first Elizabethans as to us. To find that Henry does not display the attractive personal qualities and waywardness of Prince Hal is to erect a barrier to one's appreciation. That indeed is what often happens to learned critics, as one can see from Dr. Tillyard's *Shakespeare's History Plays*, 1950. He considers that Shakespeare jettisoned the character he had created in the Prince:

D*

. . . substituting one which, though lacking all consistency, satisfied the requirements both of the chroniclers and of popular tradition. No wonder if the play constructed round him shows a great falling off in quality.

I do not think Shakespeare was doing anything of the kind, and the conclusion to which the critic comes, that the play falls off, cannot be maintained. He was writing a drama of an English hero-king, and chose Henry as a popular figure. He had no concern with the chroniclers except to borrow from them as it suited him, and was indifferent to their demands, because his aim was different; he was writing drama, not history. The play is a different kind of work, with in some respects different aims from the two Henry plays that preceded it. Though, as in all the history plays, the unscrupulousness of politicians has a large part, it has to be judged on its own terms as a patriotic drama in honour of England. On those terms, I suggest, there is no falling off in dramatic quality, for Shakespeare had not attempted the same thing before.

If the play is looked at as the vision of the hero who invites the audience to participate in his experience as he imaginatively conceives it, an altogether different point of view is established from that often maintained by scholars. I suggest that to be the correct standpoint from which the play should be approached.

Of its kind the play is altogether successful. If one loves one's country (and to lovers of their country the play is addressed), it fires the heart:

> O for a Muse of Fire, that would ascend
> The brightest Heaven of Invention . . .

is how the Prologue opens. The audience is intended to be highly expectant, making itself ready for no ordinary drama, invited to set free its imagination, and to:

> Peace out our imperfections with your thoughts.

The Chorus appears before each act to stir up the audience, and Henry's long speeches, in 2.2, 3.1, 4.1 and 3, are directed to the audience, and intended to excite and move those who are sharing in the play. It is indeed a tremendous work.

Without question the play is increased in dramatic force by keeping the King central throughout, including, in imagination, the scenes in which he does not appear, by hearing his voice in the

Chorus, and by seeing the entire action through his eyes. That gives everything clarity and definition. The account of Falstaff's end (2.3) is Henry's account of what happened, stated in the terms of his vision; that is why it is so touching. It is said that Shakespeare had to kill Falstaff because the play was not large enough to contain him: in fact the play's theme is antagonistic to that gross man. In the same critical vein is Leigh Hunt's declaration that the play "comprises little of the humanity that fills most of the plays", which was spoken from the heart of a naturalistic critic. Note that Falstaff's rejection is followed by the condemnation of the traitors, "the mercy that was quicke in us . . . is supprest and kill'd. . . ."

The French king and his forces before, during and after the battle are as Henry presents them, so are the amazing Fluellen and Pistol, and so is the wooing of the French Princess. In this lies the integrity of the play, and its quality as great drama. The falsity of the argument for war and the evils of war when waged are not glossed over but made plain with contempt for the one and shame for the other.

AS YOU LIKE IT (1599)

In this play the hint in *Much Ado* is acted upon, and a woman protagonist appears. For the first time, it seems to me, the function of the protagonist is fully carried out with not the slightest faltering, and from now on Shakespeare is always sure of his dramatic method. This play demonstrates that he was completely master of the law of drama. It is curious that there are no records of its performance, except for one uncertain entry in Shakespeare's time, until the mideighteenth century. Since then it has always been popular.

It is a play of unalloyed happiness. Whatever sadness there is in it is fleeting, its spirit being contained in the lines:

> Come hither, come hither, come hither,
> Heere shall he see no enemie.

> (2.5)

"We are fleeting the time carelessly," remarked Quiller-Couch, and he goes on to add that it is "not . . . a drama, but . . . a dream, or rather a dreamy delicious fantasy, and especially a fantasy of colour". This is an example of the sentimental writing devoted to Shakespeare which is called criticism. Certainly the play is a dream but not the careless work that the critics find it, and certainly it is "a drama". The only serious character in Quiller-Couch's opinion is Adam, and he actually declares that "Rosalind herself is not perfect", while he can scarcely bring himself to mention the "piece of mere botchwork . . . I mean the introduction of Hymen in the last Act".

I refer to this criticism not for the sake of continuing a quarrel with an eminent and long since dead scholar, but because it is characteristic of Shakespeare criticism in general, in which, because the nature of the work criticized is clouded by pre-conceptions and a false idea of the nature of drama, the criticism is beside the mark. The theme of this play is happiness: happiness in love, happiness in marriage. It is "as you like it", as the title says. Bernard Shaw as dramatic critic professed to dislike it for lack of social content, and went on:

> Shakespeare . . . had to take a popular novel; make a shallow, unnatural, indulgent, pleasant, popular drama of it; and hand it to the theatre with no hint of his feelings except the significant title, As You Like It. And we have not even the wit to feel the snub.

As this was written of a London performance that rightly displeased him it can be excused; the truth is that Shaw was not lacking in appreciation of the play. What, indeed, can be more pleasing than for one's desires to be satisfied? That is what happens: everyone in the play gets his heart's desire, though not in the way at first looked for. What more perfect close could there be to a play about marriage than the presence of the god of marriage, Hymen himself? His words justify his appearance:

> Then is there mirth in heaven,
> When earthly things made even,
> Atone together.
> (5.4)

"Mirth" is "happiness", and heaven's happiness is one with earth's in the atonement of marriage that "ends in true delights".

The play is Rosalind's reflection upon and recapitulation of the events with which it deals. Her problem is how to be united with Orlando. She solves the problem, of course, and all that takes place in her vision, which is the play, is from the point of view of its solution. Orlando is the perfect lover, not an ordinary, good looking, poetical young man, but an ideal lover, without a flaw in everything he says and does, and it is specially to be noted that never once does he do or say anything with which fault can be found. The scenes between him and Rosalind, when he, blinded in his mind's eye by recollection, is induced to make love to her without realizing who she is—for he never looks at her—are exquisite. And when played as they should be, with Rosalind controlling the situation, everyone moving in dream, the delight they give is intense.

The play is mostly in prose, but the prose is poetic, not the prose of the non-dramatic. The speaking requires elevation of diction. It is to be noted that when Rosalind is not on the stage, everything is heightened, made more grotesque or more moving, and sometimes is more simply poetical than when she is present.

There are those—most of the critics—who quarrel with Touchstone's marriage with the wench, Audry, and Oliver's marriage with Celia. Both were necessary. Touchstone, though full of wise words, is also a fool; it is his profession and he acts accordingly: his marriage is folly, as he says. As the object of the play is reconciliation and happiness, the wicked Oliver had to repent, be converted, and join with the others. To find fault with this marriage on naturalistic grounds is to fail to appreciate poetic values.

Jacques is the one character not reconciled, for he represents worldly wisdom and his presence gives a touch of astringency. He is the exact opposite of Rosalind, and is there for that purpose. But he takes pains to give the lovers his blessing before he goes.

THE THIRD PERIOD
(1599-1607)

Julius Caesar—The Merry Wives of Windsor—Troilus and Cressida—Hamlet—Twelfth Night—All's Well that Ends Well—Measure for Measure—Othello—Macbeth—King Lear—Anthony and Cleopatra—Coriolanus—Timon of Athens.

THERE are thirteen plays to be considered in this section, including the great tragedies. With the exception of two of the plays we see Shakespeare working unmistakably within the law of drama. In *As You Like It*, he had shown that he was master of the law and these plays confirm it. The grandeur of the tragedies is overwhelming, and that they are dramatically and in the mind of the poet related to each other cannot be overlooked. One approaches them with an utter sense of inadequacy, for a critic should be able to stand on the level of the work criticized, which is impossible here.

The period covered by the writing of these plays is eight years. It may have been less. In what state of mind and soul must Shakespeare have been during that time? He had practical affairs to look after, the theatre, his property, his family and his friends, and was engaged in rehearsing and getting one play staged while another was being written. We know nothing about him except for unimportant items of information, and what the works themselves provide. What a life it must have been with these plays as its product! We are left to study the plays, to perform them, and to participate in their performance.

We see in them indications of the arduous process through which Shakespeare had to go to find his own depth as a dramatist. They are records of strenuous effort, not simply that required to write the particular works but to give form to the world as he knew it to be, and to his own inner life, of which the entire works provide the unique testimony. We know from the Sonnets how dissatisfied he was with his work; he was not a merely happy and genial man but a man of suffering, as these thirteen plays abundantly show.

They provide evidence, which I do not see how anyone can refute, of the "law" of drama as I have attempted to define it. They support it, I venture to suggest, in every particular, and the second of the plays, in which it is not observed, shows the kind of theatrical work that results when that takes place. I do not think Shakespeare was concerned with drama in that play and knew very well what he was doing.

THE TRAGEDY OF JULIUS CAESAR (1599)

There is no play that so clearly demonstrates that Shakespeare was not writing history as *Julius Caesar*, for this play treats history as merely the raw material for drama. Not that Shakespeare falsifies history, which he never does; he places emphasis not upon history, as such, but upon a dramatic situation of universal significance. The play's hero is not Julius Caesar, as we should expect from its title, but another : Caesar provides the occasion or situation for the tragedy. He appears in the last days of his career, at a moment of personal weakness and political crisis, when the republican plot against him became successful. His removal was long prepared; it had involved civil war, and his aim of replacing the dictatorship of the republic by being crowned king was on the point of achievement. His murder was one of Rome's decisive days. Shakespeare is not careless about the main facts and does not misrepresent them, but his interest is in the heart and mind of Brutus, one of the leading conspirators. He enlarges him into the protagonist, taking his character from Plutarch, who said that Brutus was :

> . . . esteemed of noblemen, and hated of no man, not so much as of his enemies : because he was a marvellous lowly and gentle person, noble-minded, and would never be in a rage, nor carried away with pleasure and covetousness, but had ever an upright mind with him, and would never yield to any wrong or injustice, the which was the chiefest cause of his fame, of his rising, and of the good-will that every man bare him; for they were all persuaded that his interest was good.

Even if the real man did not possess these qualities it does not matter, for Shakespeare's intention is to concentrate attention upon what happens to a man of principle who engages in politics, how he fails, the disaster that overtakes him, and how in death he is reconciled with eternity.

Furthermore, Shakespeare was concerned not with Romans but with Englishmen. Goethe put it tersely:

> You will hear that he describes Romans wonderfully; I do not think so: they are flesh and blood Englishmen; but at any rate they are men from top to toe, and the Roman toga sits well on them.

Our attention is not intended to be directed to ancient Rome, but here at home, to ourselves, to our time, to our own land.

This is the first Shakespeare tragedy in which the law of drama has perfect recognition. From that point of view the play has no flaw. It is indeed a most impressive work, and has always been so recognized.

Yet it has to be admitted that there are reasons for the critics' qualified acceptance of the popular recognition of the play, for Brutus is acknowledged by them as the hero only grudgingly, and much fault is found in him. To begin with, Shakespeare does not display him as lovable. He is cultivated, but cold in his moral rectitude; it seems certain that this coldness was deliberately aimed at by the dramatist. His icy idealism, the high level of moral principle upon which he stands, is necessary for Shakespeare's object, and why should critics demand a Brutus in their own image? Men of rectitude and high moral principle are seldom lovable. There can be little doubt that Shakespeare intended to show the effect that politics, which for practical ends often requires that evil be done, has upon a man of principle.

Those critics who cannot stand Brutus, which includes Granville Barker, and among the latest Mr. H. B. Charlton, are in difficulty. Says Mr. Charlton:

> The Brutus of Julius Caesar is incapable of moulding the whole play to a tragic pattern.

But the criticism holds no water, for when the play is examined in the context of the law of drama, its integrity as tragedy is unmistakable, and the work approached perfection.

Perhaps because he did not like Brutus, Granville Barker found three protagonists in the play, Brutus, Cassius, and Antony, which is equivalent to finding none. Yet he has to come down on the side of Brutus's pre-eminence in the play and says:

> We find in it . . . a stagecraft bold and free.
> We may here study Elizabethan stagecraft, as such, almost if not quite at its best.

Without a distinguishable protagonist, however, there is no stage-craft, for wherein does the essential element in stagecraft lie but in the presentation of a protagonist and the dramatic action in which his problem is contained? There can, I think, be no doubt that Brutus is the protagonist, and most critics have so recognized him.

He declares himself and states his problem in his opening scene with Cassius:

> I turne the trouble of my Countenance
> Meerely upon myselfe.
> (1.2)

At the end of the scene he is described by Cassius in admirable terms, for the protagonist has to be fully presented. Throughout the play Brutus, the idealist, is contrasted with Cassius, the realist politician, though the astute Antony provides the turning point of the action; for it is Brutus's mistake, first, in not allowing Antony to suffer Caesar's fate, secondly in allowing him to address the citizens, that brings about his downfall. The Brutus-Cassius episode (4.3), one of the most highly praised dramatic scenes in Shakespeare, has also been declared to be superfluous to the action. Bradley thought so, though he admitted that it provides relief to the tension. Its object is, however, to present another side of Brutus's fundamental quarrel with Cassius. Those who object to it look at the plot as usual from a naturalistic point of view.

The excellent John Palmer thought Shakespeare was presenting in Brutus a politician unfit for politics, instead of, as I think, what happens when a man does wrong with good motives—the wrong destroys him. Had Brutus been astute he would have avoided any such outcome. But such astuteness and virtue do not go together. It was not Antony's astuteness, however, so much as the evil in himself that brought about Brutus's downfall. For murder is evil. He never rids his mind of Caesar, his ghost appears to him, and over the bodies of Cassius and Titinius he says:

> O Julius Caesar, thou art mighty yet,
> Thy spirit walks abroad, and turnes our Swords
> Into our owne proper entrailes.
> (5.3)

His last words are:

> Caesar, now be still:
> I kill'd not thee with halfe so good a will.
> (5.5)

The difficulties of the play pointed out by Granville Barker and others, which they account for by clumsy workmanship and otherwise, are entirely cleared up when the requirements of the law of drama are perceived. The action is simultaneous, and there is, except for stage verisimilitude and for the sake of concreteness, no time or place to be observed, for everything is immediately present. Therefore no difficulty should occur over the important soliloquy in 2.1 which so bothered Coleridge, "What character does Shakespeare mean his Brutus to be?" asked he with horror, echoed in the writings of many other critics, including Granville Barker, who excused Shakespeare for "still fumbling" though perhaps Brutus was "fumbling too", and Mr. Charlton who calls it "muddle-headedness" and "the intellectual fuddles of a man whose heart is good". What Brutus says in that scene is:

It must be by his death.

(2.1)

though he has not yet been invited to join the conspirators. The explanation is that the action of the play is presented from the standpoint of its end. There is no need to apologize for Brutus's betrayal of Caesar by saying that he was led astray by the conspirators: this speech ought to be understood as making clear that it was Brutus's sense of the wrong to liberty that might follow from Caesar becoming greater in power than he was already that brought him to the conclusion that ambition must be killed "in the shell". In this self-revelation we see the course of events to come.

Shakespeare was ever against tyrants, and that the tyrant must die for the sake of liberty was perceived by him as necessary. Yet the clear-eyed Shakespeare also saw that to do evil for the sake of good brought worse evils than were desired to be removed; for, the tyrant being killed, the tyranny continues, and another civil war is the outcome.

A further source of critical trouble occurs in 4.3 which contains two references to Portia's death. Brutus already knew of her death, for he tells Cassius of it before he gets the message from Messala, yet he receives that message with obvious surprise. Pages of discussion have been devoted to explaining this apparent prevarication. Granville Barker thought it might be due to something wrong with the text, or perhaps simply caused by "the vagaries of a playwright's mind". The truth is, I suggest, that this is evidence of the play as

vision and that Portia had died and Brutus knew the fact before
the dramatic action with which the play is concerned has begun.

The self-description of Julius Caesar in 2.2 should be regarded as
Brutus's own thoughts, though the words are spoken by Caesar. This
is how Brutus saw the "colossus". The American critic H. N. Hudson
said "I have sometimes thought that the policy of the drama may
have been to represent Caesar not as he was indeed, but as he may
have appeared to the conspirators. . . ." He was not far from the
truth. Cassius, too, is as Brutus saw him, so is Anthony. These are
important points to keep in mind when studying the play and
producing it.

The second part of the play is declared to be weaker than the
first by many critics; but that is because they look for naturalistic
story-telling and have no idea of drama. As drama, the second part
is among the best ever written in its subtle and profound opening
of the human heart.

Granville Barker called the play "the gateway through which
Shakespeare passed to the writing of his five great tragedies", and
so indeed it is, for the rare quality of dramatic treatment given to
it he perfected in them.

THE MERRY WIVES OF WINDSOR (1600)

This popular theatrical piece is one of the exceptions among the
works of Shakespeare in the sense that it has no protagonist. Shakespeare is said to have written it at the Queen's command. The
question, "Why did he write it?" has often been asked, for the play
has seemed to need justification, and does not explain itself. The
answer is that in it Shakespeare disposes of Falstaff, one of his most
successful characters. The public has always loved Falstaff, and,
because of that love, Shakespeare, we must suppose, had to show
what he really thought of him. So here, in this play, Shakespeare
displays the selfish, stupid, dirty, cowardly old rogue made a fool of
by women. No one could be more contemptible than Falstaff is here.
There is not a good word for him in the entire play: human as he
is in the other plays and likeable at the distance of imagination, in
this play we are not intended to admire him. We are reminded
instead that Shakespeare's works are not concerned with the natural
man but with his transformation. Falstaff is the essence of natural

man, completely earthly, and Shakespeare rejects him. None the less Falstaff is rightly regarded as one of the dramatist's greatest creations. Shakespeare's art comprehended all men, the natural man, the outer man, the man of appetite and the world, as well as men of innerness and the spirit; but he did not mistake them. In this play he as much as says, There is your hero in his grossness, the man who prefers "life" to honour! There is no protagonist, for we are not invited to enter into Falstaff's mind, to share his experience, so that it is no more than a comic entertainment.

Certainly Falstaff has a problem—how to satisfy his appetites— but let us observe that he makes no invitation to the audience to participate. Indeed, the audience does not share anything with Falstaff, and does not laugh with him, but at him. There could be no participation in the vision of a creature who sees only himself eating, drinking, whoring, stealing, and ignoring the world beside.

Those who love Falstaff most are uneasy about this play, as they should be. Bradley considered him to be a different character from that appearing in the Henry IV plays with the same name. Quiller-Couch also says that this "is not the same man . . . he is somehow not our Falstaff", and turns quickly from him. The fault is, he supposes, that Shakespeare put him into an Italian comedy: "the plot of the *Merry Wives* is pure Italian", he declares, and Falstaff was too English a character for that. Tolstoy found Falstaff "the only natural and typical character depicted by Shakespeare", but that was because he looked for natural life and the representation of actual events in the plots of plays.

Falstaff says:

> I do begin to perceive that I am made an Asse....
> 'Tis time I were choak'd with a peece of toasted Cheese.

which was what Shakespeare intended, and we laugh at him as a figure to be ridiculed. Shakespeare seems to say, This is the contemptible man that you so love! So—

> Fie on shamefull phantasie : Fie on Lust, and Luxurie :
> Lust is but a bloudy fire, kindled with unchaste desire,
>   Fed in heart whose flames aspire,
>   As thoughts do blow them higher and higher.
> Pinch him (Fairies) mutually: Pinch him for his villanie.
>   Pinch him, and burne him, and turne him about,
> Till Candles, and Star-light, and Moone-shine be out.

(5.5)

And his last words are:

> Well I am your Theame: you have the start of me;
> I am dejected: I am not able to answer.

> (5.5)

Thus he fades away. For perhaps Shakespeare ironically wants us to understand that the greatest wonders of Nature unlike the works of poetry pass away to be seen no more.

THE TRAGEDY OF TROILUS AND CRESSIDA (1600)

About this play there is much argument. It is found in the First Folio between the Histories and the Tragedies, without pagination, and without appearing in the "Catalogue of Contents", and where it comes in Shakespeare's career is uncertain. It was entered on the Stationers' Register in 1603, and the first Quarto published in 1609 said that it was acted at the Globe, while a second Quarto published the same year by the same printers declared that it was "never stal'd with the Stage". Critics think other people had a hand in it. Coleridge found it a hard play. Hazlitt thought it "loose and desultry". Quiller-Couch ignored it.

Probably it was written for a special occasion and never performed at the Globe, if at all. It is an odd play, "neither tragedy, comedy, nor history", says Dr. Tillyard, and he is right. In the Quarto it was entitled *The History of Troilus and Cressida*, which is nearly equivalent to calling it a narrative. Whenever there is trouble about a play it is invariably due to uncertainty about the protagonist or to his being weakly presented. That is what is wrong here. Who is the protagonist? He could be Hector or Ulysses or Troilus. Hector is the noblest, Ulysses the ablest, Troilus the most poetic. Hector is undoubtedly a great man, and in the debate between Priam and his sons he shows quality of intellect; at the end he is murdered. He has the dimensions and character of a tragic hero, except that he is unclear and has a divided mind. Ulysses is the leader of the Greeks, and his great speech on the "specialty of Rule", regarded by some as the central feature of the play, puts him in what seems a premier position; but though he may be first among the Greeks he cannot by any stretch of imagination be considered the first in the play, even though the tragedy might be that he, too, is murdered. The play ends with Troilus's speech on the murder, the final words by Pandarus being in the nature of an epilogue. He, Troilus, who lends his name to the play, is the one who most nearly satisfies what is required in a protagonist. His is the problem, his love for Cressida (which Coleridge praised so highly), and of all the characters he is the most active and the man of finest nature. He is thus described by Ulysses:

> The youngest Sonne of Priam;
> A true Knight; they call him Troylus;
> Not yet mature, yet matchless, firme of word,
> Speaking in deedes, and deedlesse in his tongue;
> Not soone provok't, nor being provok't, soon calm'd;
> His heart and hand both open, and both free:
> For what he has, he gives; what thinks, he shewes;
> Yet gives he not till judgement guide his bounty,
> Nor dignifies an impure thought with breath:
> Manly as Hector, but more dangerous;
> For Hector in his blaze of wrath subscribes
> To tender objects; but he, in heate of action,
> Is more vindicative than jealous love.

(4.5)

Yet Troilus is unsatisfactory. On the background of the war between Greece and Troy, which is a momentous affair, there is his romantic love affair, not at all momentous, though with this theme the play opens. As a lover, Troilus cuts by no means a good figure, being helpless in the hands both of Cressida and dire necessity. He has her but has to let her go; then she shews herself wanton. This could make him a protagonist in a comic sense; but that does not seem intended, and the play has not the spirit of comedy. As a leader among the Trojan commanders Troilus is an idealist, and invites defeat, lacking any sort of political intelligence which does not commend him. Reason that should guide Troilus is "bi-fold", so that he understands neither himself nor his problem. Furthermore, he is out of the action far too much to be satisfactory as a protagonist, and the action relevant to the plot is remote from him. This is a serious dramatic weakness, and accounts for the relative failure of the play; for while it is possible to conceive of the action in the terms of Troilus's vision and to accept the play as a statement through his eyes, it is not possible to feel his presence throughout. He is talked about during the Greek discussions from which the speech by

Ulysses just quoted comes, but the atmosphere is not his: it remains strange to him, he is outside it. This is contrary to what is to be expected in a protagonist, who must incorporate opposites in himself and reconcile the contraries, which Troilus never does. When the third scene of the first act opens and we are clearly in another world from that of Troilus in Troy, a diversion is immediately created, which causes the "inflation and deflation", of which Dr. Tillyard speaks, though he puts it down to the alternating verse and prose; but he rightly says:

> Our responses are thus complicated; and not every spectator likes to be thus played on.

I do not think the changes between verse and prose have anything to do with it, for the prose is not mere prose. It is the fact that the play lacks the essential unity that only a protagonist can give, which accounts for its weakness. Thus the participation of the audience is hindered, which is fatal to drama. Though the play makes an admirable spectacle, contains erotic excitement, much comedy, and at times stirring action, none of these elements remedies that defect. Yet having fathomed all our doubts we must conclude that Troilus is the protagonist; unless that is accepted, whatever the difficulties and no matter the weaknesses, the play does not make sense.

I should add that in my view Dr. Tillyard's discussion of the play, in the book from which I have quoted, is the best that has recently been done. Professor Wilson Knight has an important essay on the play in The Wheel of Fire, in which he finds the central ideal of the play in the opposition of two aspects of life:

> The Trojan party stands for human beauty and worth, the Greek party for the bestial and stupid elements of man, the barren stagnancy of intellect divorced from action, and the criticism which exposes these things with jeers.

As it is no part of my present business to consider the play apart from the specific point of view this book is written to sustain, I cannot discuss Professor Knight's interesting argument; but it seems clear from the exposition of what he regards as a masterly work that the play must be regarded as a failure, for he admits at the end of the essay that, "the consciousness of Troilus is wrenched, divided".

If that be so, as indeed it is, the function of Troilus as protagonist, which ought to be nothing less than reconciliation, unity, or illumination, has not been fully discharged. That is sufficient for our present purpose; and no admiration for its intellectual content can raise the play on to the level of a successful dramatic work. Professor Ellis-Fermor appeared to confuse the play's weakness with weakness of theme in her comments in *The Frontiers of Drama* (1945). She thought the play put forward the inherent sickness of human nature, though its inherent weakness is rather in the presentation of the protagonist. The dramatist has miscarried, not having achieved what he intended.

Why this should be we do not know, but an examination of the play with this in mind might disclose interesting evidence throwing light upon Shakespeare as dramatist, and upon the nature of drama in general. That this is an important work, defective as it is, there can be no gainsaying.

THE TRAGEDY OF HAMLET, PRINCE OF DENMARK (1601)

How does it happen that this is the most closely studied, most widely played, most undeniably popular, and the most appealing play of Shakespeare's to all men, everywhere? The question is of great interest, and what I say here is an attempt to provide an answer, which, to put it shortly, is that the play provides the most perfect example of the "law" of drama in the world.

That Hamlet is the protagonist there is no question, and that he has a problem is clear enough, though what the problem is is not so clear. Indeed *Hamlet* is the supreme example of a problem play, for a library of books has been published about that one point. Never has any play proved so puzzling. Though as I contend every play is a problem play, this presents a problem of such a nature that one of the latest and most learned critics, Dr. Tillyard (*Shakespeare's Problem Plays*, 1950), will not have it that it is a tragedy at all! His definition of a tragedy includes three types (1) suffering that befalls a strong nature, for which the hero is at least partly responsible, (2) sacrificial purgation, and (3) removal consequent upon destruction, none of which he thinks applies to *Hamlet*. All the same, he calls the play:

> . . . the greatest display of sheer imaginative vitality in literary form that a man has so far achieved.

One accepts this statement wholeheartedly, but unlike Dr. Tillyard I think Hamlet to have been responsible for his tragic fate, also that he changed and was redeemed, which makes it what it is.

Although the action of the play can easily be followed, it is true that apart from its central problem a certain obscurity arises in almost every episode. Exactly what is happening, or why, we are never sure from the first scene when the Ghost appears to the last when the stage is strewn with corpses. There can be little doubt that this obscurity was no accident. It is not necessary to suppose that it was due to faulty workmanship, and we can assume that obscurity was intended; for the art of drama is not merely to tell a story, but to involve the audience in the action, and what more certain way could there be of bringing this about than to make the audience wonder, to tantalize it with doubt from moment to moment, so that it must think steadily about what is happening, and thus become increasingly active in participation? The principle of ambiguity is well recognized in art, of which perhaps the popular example is Leonardo da Vinci's "Mona Lisa", and the great poets, among them Coleridge and Keats, constantly followed it. (As for the moderns in poetry, painting and music, I say only that they seem to press it for all it is worth.) In *Hamlet* the obscurity exists because more than the audience's emotions are engaged; for the play calls insistently for mental collaboration. What Dr. Dover Wilson says is to the point:

> Hamlet is a dramatic essay in mystery; that is to say it is so con-
> structed that the more it is examined the more there is to discover.

The books that are written and the perpetual discussion about the play are witness to the dramatist's aim. Though seemingly straight-forward—the plot so very simple that the play could be made into a film—by no means difficult to perform upon the stage, and crystal-clear compared with the last play we considered, the play is immensely perplexing. That, indeed, is part of its unending delight.

Let us, then, consider what was Hamlet's problem. That it was a problem involving indecision everyone is agreed. "A man who would not make up his mind" is an easy and popular description of the character. Everyone knows from experience that to make up one's mind upon an indicated course of action is often a hard matter; but that is too trivial a problem for a tragic theme. Merely to struggle with the difficulty of making a decision does not cause a character to be admirable; it might easily bring him into contempt. If Hamlet's problem were simply one of indecision he would be no hero, and would be undeserving of the world's attention. Indeed, Hazlitt (1817) found him to be "as little of the hero as a man well could be", for he was "incapable of deliberate action", he "dallies with his purposes", and "because he cannot have his revenge perfect . . . he declines it". A more severe judgement it would be hard to make. Yet the world is fascinated by this "weak" young man, so that it is worth while to search for the cause of his apparent vacillation. What Hamlet is required to make up his mind about is plain enough: to avenge his father's murder. His father's Ghost reveals to him that he was murdered, and demands revenge, and Hamlet agrees to carry out the Ghost's bidding. But he hesitates; he does not act. Why?

Every possible answer has been given to the question. Samuel Johnson (1765) considered Hamlet to be, throughout the play, rather an instrument than an agent, an idea taken up by G. S. Gordon (1912) who declared, "It is Fate . . . that is the driving genius of the play and winds it to its end". Coleridge (1818) thought Hamlet a young intellectual who merely procrastinates, though called by "every motive human and divine" to his revenge, while Bradley (1904) found him to be neurotic, suffering from melancholia, unable to take action in a practical situation. Dover Wilson (1932) combines the faults in defect of character. These are the favourite explanations, repeated over and over again, with inclinations towards an abnormal mother attachment, or doubts about Ophelia. The Spanish critic, Señor Madariaga, in one of the most witty and skilful studies of the play, seeks to prove that Hamlet is egocentric:

. . . The centre of Hamlet's interest, thought, motive and emotion is his own self. . . .

For that reason he cannot bring himself "to commit that individual crime which is a social execution". This is put in another way in the study provided by Miss M. D. Parker in her book, The Slave of Life (1955), when she says that "the reason Hamlet cannot kill Claudius is that he spends his time thinking about universal corruption", describing him as "a man who knows too much for the world he lives in but not enough for the real world". While Mr. Brent Stirling thinks Hamlet's trouble to be "a sense of underemotion [which] leads to overemotion". (Unity in Shakespearean Tragedy 1956). Wilson Knight's reconsidered judgement (1947) is that it is "a play of death". All these are no more than variations of the neurosis explanation.

Professor Wilson Knight does, indeed, give attention to the play on the spiritual level "in a highly complex analysis", but still does not find it one of consciousness, that is to say, conscience. Mr. F. L. Lucas dismisses the factor of conscience in favour of a psycho-analytical explanation in *Literature and Psychology* (1951), because he considers that Hamlet never questions "the rightness of revenge". But, indeed, he does, and surely Mr. Lucas is wrong in supposing that the Elizabethan audience did not question it. Although it is true that there was conflict of practice in Elizabethan England, as there is today, for in politics revenge still plays an active part, every Elizabethan knew that revenge was a mortal sin, and Shakespeare took that knowledge for granted, as all Christendom did. Certainly the motive of revenge is strong throughout the play: not only does the Ghost display it but Claudius acts upon it, so does Laertes. Every man is tempted to revenge wrongs, and Shakespeare's play is for all men. Hamlet, however, does not yield to the temptation.

Conscience is the source of Hamlet's problem. He did not live in dream but was a conscious man. Bradley mentions, only to reject the view, that Hamlet was restrained by moral scruple, and considers that "attention to the text is fatal to it". My own opinion is that Bradley is wrong about the text, which supports the view that Hamlet does not carry out the Ghost's bidding because he is not convinced that revenge is his moral duty. The Ghost, thirsting for revenge, said, Do it. The whole world of natural men echo the poor Ghost. What alternative had Hamlet, as a natural man, to revenging his father's murder? He had none. The point of the play is that Hamlet is a civilized man and a Christian. To such a man revenge is at least questionable. There is a scene in the First Quarto omitted in the Folio, but contained in modern texts (4.4), which contains Hamlet's self-accusing soliloquy, "How all occasions do inform against me", which shows him fighting against himself: is he afraid of "bestiall oblivion", or has his conscience made a craven of him? He is very doubtful, for he sees "honour at the stake", finds no justification for his behaviour, and ends the speech lamely. The play is better without it, as the original editors (and perhaps Shakespeare) knew. It does, however, show that conscience was his problem: "thinking too precisely on th' event", and confirms my argument. The play, however, is not argument or philosophy, but

the drama of a man convinced. He has already said, "Thus Conscience does make Cowards of us all", which is the play's central
utterance. He speaks about conscience again at the end referring to
his treatment of Guildensterne and Rosencrance—"They are not near
my conscience". His situation as a civilized man, confronted with
this problem, is the very action of the play; this the audience is
expected to see. I think the Elizabethan audience did see it; though
a brutal age, and in our sense unrefined, the idea of the wrongfulness
of murder was familiar; and whether it was morally permissible,
and under what conditions, to answer murder with murder, were
questions into which those who made up the audience could readily
enter. The problem of conscience was not a small thing to them
but belonged to the tragic character of the time, when problems of
conscience were acutely before every man in religion and in politics.
Indeed, opposition to private justice, or revenge, is fundamental in
Western Christianity, one of its characteristic and most certain
postulates. The Church was ceaselessly engaged in the struggle against
revenge, which was unquestionably a sin. It can be said that this
complete rejection of revenge belongs to the basis of Western civili-
zation, and in this the importance of *Hamlet* undoubtedly lies.

What happens in the play is most emphatically not what Goethe
said :

> . . . a lovely pure and moral nature, without the strength of nerve
> which forms a hero, sinks beneath a burden which it cannot bear and
> must not cast away.

Were that true criticism, Shakespeare would not have written a
tragedy, and though Hamlet dies he does not sink beneath the
burden of his moral problem. He resolved it. At the end it is not
weakness but strength that possesses him. He is a fully conscious
hero, a mature man aware of good and evil. He had free will, which
is what makes him so fascinating a character. Hamlet's self-conscious-
ness, which fully developed is self-responsibility, is what gives the
play its absorbing interest.

At this point I want to suggest that where the critics without
exception have gone wrong, from Coleridge to Goethe and from
Bradley to Tillyard, to say nothing of Miss Parker, is that they regard
the play as a history of an actual person in the world of every-day
life, giving too little attention to the fact that it is a work of imagination. They forget that the play does not exist by legalistic, moralistic,

or naturalistic standards, only as a vision of life. Goethe could hardly
have been more wrong, and Bradley is the outstanding example
among modern critics of those who continue in his error. Hardly any
critic seems to be free from it. Bradley finds Hamlet "not far from in-
sanity", and judges him in relation to his failure to carry out a "sacred
duty", "his appointed task", and makes the sweeping condemnation :

> . . . whatever else passed in a sickening round throughout Hamlet's
> mind, was not the healthy and right deliberation of a man with such
> a task, but otiose thinking hardly deserving the name of thought, an
> unconscious weaving of pretexts for inaction, aimless tossings on a sick
> bed, symptoms of melancholy which only increased it by deepening self-
> contempt.

If that indeed were true, it would be impossible to explain the world's
profound interest in the play. Indeed, it would go towards justifying
Tolstoy's repugnance to it as "coarse, immoral, mean and senseless",
because he thought it "based on pagan revenge." Unless we can enter
into the realm in which Shakespeare set his hero, and regard him
with insight, realizing with imaginative sympathy what is happening, we shall not understand the world's interest or be capable of
criticizing the play. Madariaga perceives this, and pours scorn upon
those who naively have "identified Shakespeare's characters with
human beings" in their weakest most common-place aspects, but
proceeds to do the very thing he condemns !

What else, indeed, can any critic do unless he recognizes the
function of a tragic hero and keeps his mind steadily upon it? That
function is to present a vision of his predicament and its solution in
which the entire action appears from his final point of view. Unless
the play is examined from that standpoint, and the critic asks himself if the dramatist has carried out what he has set out to do, no
valid criticism can be made. In that sense Quiller-Couch was not
off the mark when he said of criticism of the play that "nine-tenths
of it is rubbish".

It is interesting that the critic just mentioned, who is contemptuous
of those who take for granted that it was Hamlet's duty to kill
Claudius, yet perceived that Hamlet's problem was one of conscience,
does not concentrate upon that explanation, but wanders off into
saying that the solution of the problem of Hamlet is that "each feels
'This is I' ", and is content to leave it at that. Of course, we see
ourselves in Hamlet, as in every tragic hero, but the critic's task is

to elucidate what the spectator sees, so that the vision may become clear and the delight more intense because heightened in the imagination.

Professor Wilson Knight in declaring that Hamlet does not know why he does not slay Claudius (in "Hamlet Reconsidered", 1947) makes what is not far short of an onslaught upon the play, which seems to have become distasteful to him. He would like to consider Claudius the hero, but even if it be sustained that Claudius was an admirable man, he was the reverse of it in Hamlet's eyes, and only with the character as he appears to Hamlet are we concerned. Professor Knight finds the play "inexhaustibly baffling"—as, indeed, it is on his interpretation, for it would be baffling to have as protagonist a character so morally base as Claudius.

Mr. T. S. Eliot says that "the essential emotion of the play is the feeling of a son towards a guilty mother", accepting J. M. Robertson's conclusion, but going further, for he says:

> Hamlet (the man) is dominated by an emotion which is inexpressible, because it is in *excess* of the facts as they appear.

This is to continue to criticize the play on a naturalistic basis, which leads him to the conclusion:

> We must simply admit that here Shakespeare tackled a problem which proved too much for him.

In the book to which I have referred Mr. F. L. Lucas is content to find a story in *Hamlet* and a good story, for which reason he does not agree with Mr. Eliot that the play is a failure. But to be content with the story is not sufficient, for it remains a naturalistic point of view. To disagree further with Mr. Lucas, the play does not depend upon primitive psychology, nor does it provide another example of the Oedipus-complex. That *Hamlet* depends for its understanding upon the psychology of civilized man seems hard for even the best critic to contemplate. The play remains alive because its essential problem is that of all civilized men.

I propose now to consider what I referred to at the opening of this commentary. First, that Hamlet was responsible for his tragic end. His end was involved in his problem; what brought Hamlet down was a fatal mistake. He was a man of reflection, which no one denies to be his leading characteristic. In a moment of self-realization he says:

> Give me that man
> That is not Passion's Slave, and I will weare him
> In my heart's Core: I, in my Heart of heart.
>
> (3.2)

These words are a key to the play: for he will not be the slave of natural passion, "a Pipe for Fortune's finger", but one whose "Blood and Judgement are so well commingled", that he can act in a way deserving blessing. Yet at a critical moment he does act without reflection, and kills the hidden Polonius, thinking him to be the spying Claudius. It is an interesting point that Hamlet does not appear to be concerned about the killing of Polonius, a "wretched, rash, intruding foole": he does not regard his action as murder, but as self-defence. Yet he sees its significance and says:

> . . . but heaven hath pleas'd it so
> To punish me with this.

It is his undoing, for it causes Laertes to enter the plot to murder him. Unpremeditated and rash action is often, in Shakespeare, the cause of tragedy, or near-tragedy. What is called natural reaction may be disastrous, as Lear shows in his treatment of Cordelia, and Leontes in his suspicion of his Queen.

That the hero should find redemption in disaster is a necessary element and it takes place in *Hamlet*. We see no more of Hamlet (in the Folio) after he is sent off to England at the beginning of the fourth act until he appears again in Horatio's company early in Act 5, where he finds the grave-digger at work. This is grim comedy, not low comedy as it is usually regarded on the stage, for it should not raise loud laughter. "Why may not Imagination trace the Noble dust of Alexander . . ." asks Hamlet, and, after the fighting at the grave with Laertes that follows, he indicates the change that has taken place in him, he knows his course. He is speaking to Horatio:

> Sir, in my heart there was a kinde of fighting,
> That would not let me sleepe.
>
> (5.2)

But when he saw on ship-board the mutineers in irons, his mind was made up:

> Our indiscretion sometimes serves us well,
> When our deare plots do paule, and that should teach us
> There's a Divinity that shapes our ends,
> Rough-hew them how we will.

His own mistake (in killing Polonius) had led him to where he discovered the king's designs against him, and with a clear conscience he turned the tables upon Guildensterne and Rosencrance. Critics have been bothered that Hamlet should have been so hard on these two men; but the explanation is offered:

> Why man, they did make love to this employment
> They are not neere my Conscience; their debate
> Doth by their owne insinuation grow:
> 'Tis dangerous, when the baser nature comes
> Betweene the passe, and fell incensed points
> Of mighty opposites.

The fighting in his heart was ended and his scruples of conscience cleared up. He goes on at once to say where he now stands:

> Does it not, thinkst thee, stand me now upon
> He that hath kill'd my King, and whor'd my Mother,
> Popt in between th' election and my hopes,
> Throwne out his Angle for my proper life,
> And with such coozenage; is't not perfect conscience,
> To quit him with this arme? And is't not to be damn'd
> To let this Canker of our nature come
> In further evil?

Everything becomes clear, though Bradley will not have it so: he notes "a certain change, though it is not great". It was, however, the greatest possible change. It is true that, without insight, we are left unsure, but it is not uncertain that Hamlet realized he could now act as a minister of justice: he can strike down his uncle in justice, not revenge. There are those who argue that Hamlet really has decided not to avenge his father but his own wrongs, which is Madariaga's view, following the editor Steevens, who said as much in his edition of the works in 1778. It is to be specifically noted, however, that the conviction of an accumulation of evil, spreading as from a canker, is what settles Hamlet in the moral decision to kill the King. This moral judgement becomes his cause. He is aware that it involves his own death, for he now proceeds in the lightening of the consciousness of death, though he does not indicate that he knows how death will come. He says:

> The interim's mine, and a man's life no more
> Than to say one.

After accepting Laertes's challenge, against which Horatio warns him, he expresses his ill-ease:

> ... thou wouldest not thinke how all heere about my heart.

But we should not suppose him to be concerned about his own death, only about his just cause; and he goes on in words that show his complete change of mind, his settled and sure conclusion:

> ... we defy Augury; there's a speciall Providence in the fall of a sparrow. If it be now, 'tis not to come: if it be not to come, it will be now: if it be not now, yet it will come, the readinesse is all, since no man has ought of what he leaves. What is't to leave betimes?

These are the conclusive words, "there's a speciall Providence in the fall of a sparrow"—his father fell, he will fall; it is Providence, and he can be content. At the end of the play, a dying man, he kills the King with the weapon the King had envenomed. It is complete justice: there is no murder for murder. He says:

> Had I but time (as this fell Sargeant death
> Is strick'd in his Arrest) oh I could tell you ...

What he would say we do not hear; but he adds words that have generally been misunderstood:

> Oh, good Horatio, what a wounded name,
> (Things standing thus unknowne) shall live behind me.

This is no complaint; it means that mystery will lie upon his memory, for that he acted for conscience sake may not be understood, but that he acted in an illumination of insight we are not intended to doubt.

The other characters take their places about Hamlet. All are, as Dr. Dover Wilson says, "under the spell of his ... imagination". We are not concerned with Claudius or Gertrude or Ophelia or Polonius or Horatio or Laertes as they were in themselves, and to discuss them as characters apart from their relation to Hamlet is meaningless. Claudius may have been a decent man, except for being a murderer and in some way getting in front of Hamlet at the election, but the spectator is not concerned with Claudius except as he appeared in Hamlet's eyes. He is not a monster in the play, for Hamlet's vision is not a flashback upon the events as they took place, but as he views them at the end; for that reason even Claudius is regarded with tolerance.

E

On any interpretation, the light-hearted Hamlet is never seen, for the clouds rest upon him always, though irradiated with the light of the setting sun. He is self-centred, as conscientious men are, and an egoist as they always are, and appeals to the egoist in every man.

On the stage, *Hamlet* is not a difficult play, provided it is played straightforwardly on meaning, even on mistaken meaning, even when regarded as a superior thriller, as it is by most actors and some critics. Often it is staged as melodrama, with the play sacrificed to the personality of a leading actor. For those reasons audiences are often hindered from participating in what the dramatist intended, which is to be rightly described as a religious experience. "We do not like to see our author's plays acted, least of all *Hamlet*," said William Hazlitt, adding, "There is no play that suffers so much from being transferred to the stage."

In the efforts made to clear up the mystery of the play, and to make everything clear by an actor's or director's improvements upon what the dramatist has left obscure, it is forgotten that the obvious is always excluded from great drama. When the play is allowed to speak for itself, its wonder is greater than anything even the cleverest director can achieve. Those who have seen performances of the full Folio text have been impressed by its extraordinary theatrical effectiveness, due as much to the lack of time to elaborate stage business to explain the inexplicable as to the unusual experience of getting the actual play.

It is important to remember that the action of the drama is continuous, and that time sequence is of no consequence. Granville Barker points out that Shakespeare treats Hamlet as about twenty years old at the start, but later in the play he is thirty. Regarded naturalistically what happens may have occupied a number of years, but natural time has nothing to do with events in vision: throughout, Hamlet sees himself as young.

The play is not improved by cutting and ought always to be played in full. What is sacrificed is usually mainly the Norwegian theme in which Claudius's political policy and its failure are dealt with. Denmark was being threatened by Norway, the importance of which is indicated by its being referred to at length in the first scene. These scenes are necessary to the play, as Goethe pointed out in *Wilhelm Meister* in 1784. He saw that to remove Fortinbras was to cause the play to fall asunder and he therefore re-wrote it (or projected its writing in his novel) almost entirely. The version played by Burbage was probably the original, somewhat cut. Betterton ignored Fortinbras except at the end of the play. David Garrick set out "to rescue the play from all the rubbish of the fifth act", so that Hamlet did not go to England, and at the end he and Claudius fight, the latter going mad and dying off. John Philip Kemble omitted Fortinbras altogether, and this version was continued by Charles Keen, Phelps and Irving. Forbes Robertson re-introduced Fortinbras, and Martin Harvey let him appear at the end.

To rely wholly upon the First Quarto is dangerous, for it was probably a "remembered" text not altogether true to the perform-ance; but if, indeed, it does more or less describe what the actors did, it indicates that they misunderstood Shakespeare as utterly as later actors have done. For instance, the Queen in the Folio version shows no knowledge of Claudius's crime; but in the Quarto she is shown to be against Claudius for his infamy, and undertakes to aid Hamlet:

> Hamlet, I view by that majesty,
> That knowes our thoughts, and lookes into our hearts,
> I will conceale, consent, and doe my best,
> What start again soe're thou shalt devise.

Of course, the player may have said nothing of the sort, and the Quarto may be a travesty of what was done upon the stage. It is clear that the play was not understood by all, which is not surprising.

In conclusion, I note that Dr. Dover Wilson suspects that *Hamlet* was not merely a turning point in Shakespeare's career dramatically, but also marked some sort of crisis in his relations with his company. It may have been so; but I think the crisis, a serious one, came later. A final word is that the play is the product of Shakespeare's extended powers.

TWELFTH NIGHT, OR WHAT YOU WILL (1602)

Everyone has thought well of this play, which has always been considered wholly delightful, though the critical Pepys found it "a silly play" on one occasion and on another "one of the weakest plays that ever I saw", which does not say much for Betterton and his company. In it Shakespeare returned to the idea of *As You Like It* and had a woman protagonist, though he made the play complex, not as simple a piece as the earlier work.

Its complexity is seen in the uncertainty about the protagonist, an uncertainty that, as I keep on saying, often exists in comedy. The protagonist might be Orsino, the greatest person in the play; it could be Olivia, the greatest lady. There is much that points to Orsino, for he opens and closes the play, and has a comic problem, how to win Olivia, which he never succeeds in doing; but can we imagine Orsino, the grandiloquent Duke, holding in his mind the scenes in which he is not the central figure? He is a too splendidly composed person for that; besides, those scenes do not in any way concern him. Olivia also has a problem, to reconcile herself to the death of her father and brother, which is not a comic problem, though there is a comic element in her falling in love with Cesario. She is too serious for a comic protagonist, however, and like Orsino is cut off in thought and sympathy from the scenes in which she does not appear.

All the requirements for a protagonist are satisfied in Viola. She is important in herself, and has the serious problem to recover her brother, whom she thinks dead but is alive, a problem complicated and made comic later by her love for the Duke and Olivia's love for her, both supposing her to be a boy. The action takes place around her, and though she is not present in many scenes it is possible to think of them as presented from her point of view. Furthermore, she has some of the most heart-plucking poetry in Shakespeare.

We should note that three women, Viola, Olivia and Maria, are everything in this play, for each claims respect, displays intelligence, wit, and good disposition, and is capable of decisive action. It is a play glorifying the hearts of women, though they are outshone in mere brilliance by the super-romantic Orsino, and in comic virtuosity by the quartet of men, Malvolio, Sir Toby, Sir Andrew and Feste. This is as it should be in comedy. What Mr. H. B. Charlton says contains an idea worth noting:

> With *As You Like It* and *Twelfth Night*, Shakespeare entered a world wherein the spiritual joys of living in time and space depended on, and were produced by, the way of life of women whose impulses of human kindness or human kindliness were guided by an intuitive common sense, which willingly consulted reason but resolutely refused to give it absolute authority. This they had power to do in virtue of that mysterious quality which is called their personality or character, the something or other mysteriously provided for them as the endowment with which they begin the process which humanity recognizes as being alive.

The play is alive, a shining work, glowing with poetic fervour, yet stinging the mind with sharp wit.

It is opened by Orsino in a scene that some producers either cut or move elsewhere, a scene essential to the play in the place in which it appears. Shakespeare's opening scenes are invariably important in the interpretation of the plays. These first words, "If Musicke be the food of Love", raise the play at once to the realm of fancy, love and poetic sensibility: this is no story of the courts of earthly princes. Observe that Orsino appears as a marvellous creation set on the very heights of love's passion. This is how Viola sees him, a prince devoted to love, what a woman longs for in her hero.

In the next scene the protagonist herself appears with those magic words for which the atmosphere created by the opening should have prepared us:

> What Country, Friends, is this?
> This is Illyria Ladie.
> . And what should I do in Illyria?
> My brother he is in Elizium,
> Perchance he is not drowned: what think you sailors?

When the action is begun, we are introduced to two comedians, another two appear after Viola disguised as a youth has become attached to the Duke, as the plot gently unfolds itself. Malvolio, the lady's steward, is intended to be played seriously. He arouses mirth and sympathy simultaneously as his self-importance strikes home.

On the opening of the second Act we find Sebastian, the feared lost brother of Viola, to be safe, so that the play is set for a comic issue. There is no need to go through the action. It is necessary to remember that the comic scenes have the delicacy, the sharpness, and the exaggeration of Viola's imagination. To think of or to play them naturalistically is to mistake them altogether. Malvolio is made an utter fool of, which should be the inevitable fate of self-importance, and if he is dealt with cruelly, as he is, we should remember that this is a woman's vision, in which feeling not reason predominates, and that we are being presented with vision, not reality.

Expertness in playing and singing is demanded throughout for the sake of the richness of the play's comic substance.

ALL'S WELL, THAT ENDS WELL (1604)

If the date of this play is correctly given the title may have reference to the problem of the succession to the throne, which had been solved on Queen Elizabeth's death in 1603 by the peaceful accession of James Stuart. There is no record of any performance until the mid-eighteenth century, after which it was constantly played, but it must have been acted perhaps many times before the Puritan closure, though we do not know. It rarely appeared during the nineteenth and has only seldom been seen on the stage in the present century. The reason is that the play's appeal is not pleasing, though it contains good scenes, excellent characters, much poetry and characteristic comic incident. The plot comes from Boccaccio, and is not harmonized with English taste. Apart from the matter of taste, as a dramatic work it is admirable.

Once more, though for the last time, Shakespeare has a woman protagonist. The function is not easy for a woman, so that relatively few plays are so written, though today in our feminine age it appears to be more possible than before. There is no reason to suppose that Shakespeare was handicapped in this matter by boy players, for where female protagonists were a dramatic necessity the boys were equal to the demands. It would form an interesting study to inquire how and in what way a protagonist's function can be reconciled with femininity. No doubt the explanation of there being few woman protagonists (though the Greeks found it possible) is that it is a reasoning function. The protagonist has to appeal to the audience's mind: the emotions are engaged and appeal is by no means only to the rational mind, but mental activity is called for, mental activity of the kind that embraces tolerance. We noted how Viola in the previous play treated Malvolio; her vision was not tolerant, and I take it that women dependent on their emotions are not exponents of toleration.

Dr. Tillyard in his valuable study of the play describes it as "in some sort a failure", but admits that he has never seen it performed, and adds, "I suspect that it acts far better than it reads". That is true: it is always impressive.

That Helena is heroine and protagonist there can be no question. Her problem is to get Bertram, who has no desire to be a husband, to marry her. She is determined and unscrupulous, yet a sweet and modest girl, and succeeds. She makes the play exhilarating, and the dramatist, conceiving her clearly and projecting his vision vividly, constructs through her what is just short of a masterly work.

Dr. Tillyard notes a "failure of the poetic imagination", which has some truth, though I think he is too assiduous in his search for rationality, not liking the bed-trick, or the fistula, or the obscenity, or the couplets, and he does not care about Helena's centrality, "She is no more interesting or instructive than Bertram", he protests. I prefer Stoll's ". . . she is the object of no criticism". I wish my plan in this book allowed me to discuss the play as a whole, for I find it rewarding.

It is a fact worth noting that Bertram is not idealized. He is Helena's choice, seen through her eyes, but she does not present him as an ideal lover for throughout the play he is far from that. This introduces an element of realism, which it is hardly necessary to say is never far from a dramatist concerned with concreteness, aiming to make his play convincing. It is realistic to remember that the man a woman chooses is not ideal, though she may please to see him so, as Rosalind does Orlando, and Viola her Duke. Helena, however, looks upon her man as very human, and very male: self-centred, proud, wilful, even cowardly, and finally empty. There are no disguises, and that he depends upon her is never obscured, though she is tender even foolish with him. This indubitably is a woman's view.

So regarded, much that is otherwise unacceptable presents no difficulty. There is no need to excuse Bertram. He behaves abominably, but so men are apt to do that women love, especially when women love in spite of themselves. To attempt to treat Bertram rationally as though we had a complete human being is to get into difficulties from which there is no escape, except to condemn the play. Hazlitt, who looked for truth to daily life in plays, admired Helena's treatment of Bertram and considered that "the most scrupulous nicety of female modesty is not once violated". Any such violation is, indeed, not to be expected when we recall the nature of drama, and the remark illustrates the fact that from the point of view of early nineteenth century London society there appeared much to be excused.

To regard the play as real life is to misinterpret Parolles and Helena's relations with him. He is a fool, and his talk with Helena about virginity is meant to be comic with a moral flavour. To object to the character, as does Quiller-Couch in his New Shakespeare edition, is to be over-squeamish. The dialogue was originally spoken by a boy Helena, and today Parolles is likely to be enacted by a feministic man, so that no existing audience is likely to be any more embarrassed than was the original Jacobean audience at the Globe, though the nineteenth century would not have had it so. But, who-ever speaks, the dialogue is admirable, to the point, and its obscenity is easily disgested.

That this dialogue occurs in the first scene is not without signi-ficance, for it points to the play being about virginity, as indeed it is:

> How might one do sir, to loose it to her owne liking?
>
> Let me see. Marry ill, to like him that ne'er it likes.

For a girl in love to think about virginity is not strange, and Helena is in love, unaccountably, with great obstacles against it, and the worldly-wise fool may help her. Her mind is pure then and always, and we are meant to understand nothing less. She concludes:

> Our remedies oft in ourselves do lye,
> Which we ascribe to heaven : the fated skye
> Gives us free scope, onely doth backward pull
> Our slow designes, when we ourselves are dull.
> What power is it, which mounts my love so hye—
> That makes me see, and cannot feede mine eye?
> The mightiest space in fortune, Nature brings
> To joyne like, likes; and kisse like native things.
> Impossible be strange attempts to those
> That weight their paines in sense, and do suppose
> What hath beene, cannot be. Who ever strove
> To shew her merit, that did misse her love?

This brave speech of a fine nature tells us to expect much. I think we are not disappointed.

It cannot be denied to be a weakness in the play, however, that in the last Act Helena is not seen, after a brief formal appearance in the first scene for the sake of the plot, until the very end. This creates difficulties for the audience, which depends upon the protagonist for its entry into the action of the play. Thus, lovely work as it is, the play is unsatisfactory, for when the audience is allowed to be treated perfunctorily by the protagonist the drama is not pleasing. Helena winds up the plot, which is no matter, but all the poetry has passed, which is everything. What is said against the play has some justification in this Act: it is the fault, as I think, of its source, the influence of which is rational, realistic, and, what is worse, undramatic, mere story telling.

MEASURE FOR MEASURE (1604)

This is a better play than All's Well, and here again there is a perfect heroine, with emphasis upon virginity, but the protagonist is a man. The play is strongly criticized, however, Shakespeare being thought to have tired of the work or his craftsmanship to have been at fault, "careless composition", says Sir Walter Greg. Pepys thought it a good play, but he saw Davenant's adaptation The Law Against Lovers, in which the Duke is a weary old man and Isabella marries Angelo. Coleridge considered the play to be "the most painful—say rather, the only painful—part of his genuine works". "Disgusting" and "horrible" he thought it, "with lust and damnable baseness". On the contrary, Hazlitt found it "as full of genius as it is of wisdom". Dr. F. R. Leavis considers it "a much greater play" than Othello. It has often been written about, and Coleridge's view may be contrasted with that of Professor Wilson Knight who says that:

> The play must be read, not as a picture of normal human affairs, but as a parable, like the parables of Jesus.

There is much in the play that seems to give offence, Angelo's character, the callousness of Isabella in preferring her chastity before her brother's life, the obscenities of Pompey, to mention the more outstanding blemishes, as they are considered to be. I think them to be nothing of the kind, and if we recognize the Duke not as a secondary character but as the protagonist, and the play as his vision, what is thought to be objectionable vanishes.

The initial difficulty appears to be in accepting what the Duke does. He hands over the government of the city to his most respected councillor for a period while he ostensibly goes abroad, though in fact he remains behind in disguise. This is not weakness on his part but wisdom, though we are not intended to dwell upon the Duke's reasons, for the play opens immediately with the situation created. He wants to know the truth about his city, truth that he cannot

E*

learn as its ruler, which is surely a good enough reason, for all rulers need such knowledge. Instead of employing spies or snoopers the Duke attempts to find out for himself.

He thinks well of Angelo, whom he makes his deputy:

> Moralitie and Mercie in Vienna
> Live in thy tongue and heart.

(1.1)

There can be no doubt that the Duke means what he says, and that he is not thinking of tricking or testing Angelo. He pretends to leave secretly, as of course he must, and gives the sufficient explanation:

> I love the people,
> But doe not like to stage me to their eyes:
> Though it doe well, I doe not relish well
> Their lowd applause, and Aves vehement:
> Nor do I thinke the man of safe discretion
> What do's affect it.

(1.1)

There is no need to under-estimate the Duke's motives or to darken his purpose. To the friar who gives him "secret harbour" he explains that he fears the laws are not being observed, and thinks the severity of Angelo should benefit the State.

The difficulty arises because it is thought that the Duke's real object was to spy upon Angelo, who is considered to be a villain, as Robert Bridges said, "a solid hypocrite all along". Thus the play becomes the unmasking of villainy. None of this is so; the Duke's plain reasons should be accepted, and Angelo should be acknowledged as a genuinely moral and upright man, who has the Duke's full confidence. Unless this is agreed the play becomes confused.

Once the Duke is recognized as the protagonist he is put into his rightful place, not as the mechanical manipulator of events, certainly not as one tired of authority, but as he who presents the drama. Thus the play makes sense and there is no need to go outside it for explanation. In truth, we cannot do so in the theatre but are bound to accept what is there enacted before us, and in this play everything required for the audience's participation is there. In performance, the drama wholly occupies the mind.

If that were recognized not so many meaningless questions would be asked about Isabella and her heartlessness by those who read the play in cold blood in their studies, for Isabella exists as the image of female virtue. To her nothing could be more terrible than the loss of chastity, so where is the hardness of heart in her refusal to give up her virtue to save her brother's life? On the contrary there should be horror at her brother's idea that there is nothing in such a sacrifice. Unless the importance of chastity is accepted the play becomes merely tiresome. Is not the virtue of chastity one of the qualities without which it is impossible to be truly human? To guard chastity is especially the duty of women. Isabella exists here for that purpose, and to inquire further into her life is not necessary; such speculations, if undertaken, have nothing to do with the play. Chastity is more than a merely negative sexual virtue: it is active and positive, the upholding of purity in thought and feeling whose beatitude is the vision of God. It is one of the very highest virtues, and to undervalue it is to take a low view of human nature.

Although the play operates on the measure for measure theme of the Gospel, which in the Rheims version of 1582 says:

> Judge not, that you be not judged. For in what judgment you judge, you shal be judged: and in what measure you mete, it shal be measured to you agayne. (Matthew, 7.1-2)

I suggest that judgement, important as it is, is secondary: the idea of purity is the essence of the vision and the wonder of this play. That the Duke marries Isabella at the end shows its importance.

So marvellous a character is Isabella that she might have been the protagonist; but Shakespeare, we can suppose, did not intend to repeat his experience with the previous play and court another relative failure. Thus, admirable as is Isabella, she exists only as the Duke sees her, which means that everything about her, including her devotion to the idea of purity, is heightened in the extreme. She was never an earthly woman, but as the Duke sees her she is perfection.

To return to Angelo, his function is to provide an example of rectitude that cannot stand moral strain. He, indeed, is a mortal man; and unless the character awakens sympathy in the audience composed of mortal men, or at least arouses understanding of human weakness, it has not been presented rightly. Of course, his weakness —his moral anarchy—is meant to be loathed, but Angelo as a man is not intended to be loathed, for he is not intended to be a monster, though in the eyes of purity he is; for while he proves that his heart contains unsuspected evil, so do all hearts. The Duke is severe:

> Shame to him, whose cruel striking,
> Kills for faults of his owne liking;
> Twice trebell shame on Angelo,
> To weede my vice and let his grow,
> Oh, what may Man within him hide,
> Though Angel on the outward side?
>
> (3.2)

Thus the Duke, addressing the audience, sums up the action at the end of the third Act.

The young men of fashion, Claudio and Lucio, have important secondary roles. Claudio is in the hands of the law for fornication, and under the law is condemned to death; as Isabella's brother he is not to be despised, though he displays masculine selfishness in his treatment of her. Lucio, on the contrary, is condemned to marry a whore and to be "whipt and hang'd", though mercifully let off the hanging. It is intended that the full effect of these happenings to the idle, thoughtless young men should be realized.

There is Pompey, played by the clown, who revels in evil, and speaks only to be obscene. This strong and hotly-heated exaggeration of wickedness is opposed to the lofty cold purity of Isabella. It is intended that the opposition should be felt. As it is presented through the Duke's eyes, who knows both, the evil is intended to be as loathsome as possible. Kemble, in his version, with Mrs. Siddons as Isabella, cut out the whole of the obscenity as his main improvement, which shows how little he understood the play.

It is usually said that the last Act is not successful. I admit that it is difficult to perform, and that, in particular, the change in the Duke from his own to the assumed part cannot easily be carried out, but properly handled the scene is practicable and effective. To say that Shakespeare's art failed him here is nonsense. When the Act fails, it is because it is "improved", and because the centrality of the Duke is not maintained. If the parts have been wrongly interpreted, Angelo treated as a scoundrel, Isabella a heartless virgin, and the Duke weak and uncertain, the Act will have the absurdity that critics find in it; but inherently it is composed as one of Shakespeare's great scenes. It is long and complicated, unnecessarily so, one might suppose, but the aim was complication, which is here a dramatic merit, and the end is reconciliation and forgiveness, which are complete.

THE TRAGEDY OF OTHELLO, THE MOOR OF VENICE (1604)

We arrive now at the first in the group of great tragedies. The theme of chastity prominent in the last two plays is continued in the present work, which has never ceased to be played since it was first performed. The plot is simple and straightforward, so simple that the play has been looked upon as melodrama, and it is usually played mainly for plot. Problems of treachery, dishonour and jealousy are raised, very familiar to all men, and there is no hindrance to participation even when the play is crudely performed. Thomas Rymar (1692), however, found it "a Bloody Farce, without salt or savour", and others have thought the play distasteful. Dr. F. R. Leavis finds its "obtuse and brutal egotism" to lead to an "insane and self-deceiving passion" (The Common Pursuit, 1952), and Mr. T. S. Eliot thinks "Othello succeeds in turning himself into a pathetic figure", and no more. Yet generally this tragedy of love has been highly thought of. "Nothing" said Charles Lamb, "can be more soothing, more flattering to the nobler parts of our natures. . . ." Said A. C. Bradley, "Of all Shakespeare's tragedies . . . Othello is the most painfully exciting and the most terrible". Even Tolstoy thought it "I will not say the best, but the least bad . . ." of the plays. Granville Barker considered that "the technical daring of the means to make it convincing, have no parallel". Professor Wilson Knight says, "In Othello we are faced with the vividly particular rather than the vague and unusual".

That Othello is the protagonist has been challenged by those who admire Iago as a theatrical character, or who choose to see two protagonists. This is due to inability to understand the protagonist's function, and is, indeed, blindness to the very nature of drama. If Othello is not the protagonist of this play there never was a protagonist in any play, and drama is anything you choose to make it: in short there is no art. What Wilson Knight says is precisely true:

> Othello is dominated by its protagonist. Its supremely beautiful effects of style are all expressions of Othello's personal passion.

The play is Othello's vision after his death, when, knowing the truth, he reflects upon his marriage and the destruction of his inner life, how he becomes suspicious and finally kills Desdemona. He invites the audience to participate in the image of this tragic experience. It is his vision of love self-defeated; himself, Desdemona, Iago and the rest are as they appear to him in that flash of vision, not as they were in themselves, or appeared at the time. In that sense, this is one of the most complete tragedies.

Consider the play from this point of view. See that Desdemona appears as an angel of purity; she says and does nothing wrong at any moment throughout the play. She loves her husband, and stands by him against her father and the world; she is incapable of doubting Othello or distrusting him; even in her death she is angelic; she is perfect. This is how Othello sees her. Iago is a monster; every thought, word and act is evil: he plots, he loves to destroy, he thinks nothing of honour, he is consumed with jealousy. He is the typical young man of the world, but worse, for he outwardly pretends to virtue. Othello himself is a soldier with his mind on his profession and his duty to the State; he loves his wife, is honourable, truthful, devoted, trustful. Despite his love, he is a lonely man, for a commander is necessarily lonely. How distant Othello is from all the men around him, even from the one he loves so purely! He struggles with his problem in loneliness, and in loneliness is overcome. It should especially be noted that he is a completely successful commander, for that is what gives the tragedy its sharp point. He is farseeing in war, able in strategy, one who plans and executes his plans. Yet he is blind to what concerns his own life most intimately; and this blindness allows his undefended soul to be undermined. Othello is young, in his prime, admirable in every worldly sense, but defeated by his very qualities, for sincerity and self-confidence bring him down. There is no flaw in him, except the one devastating, inexcusable, fatal flaw of doubting Desdemona, and the rashness of unwisdom in permitting his honour to be attacked. That is the vision: brilliant, harsh and terrible in the burning light of Vienna and Cyprus. It is, indeed, a tremendous play.

I think the play becomes more poignant and more beautiful when regarded wholly from Othello's point of view. Instead of a mere story, it becomes a man's heart opened, a revelation of the inner thought and feeling of a noble nature. It is the man himself who speaks, from the opening words, "Never tell me, I take it most un-

kindly", to the closing, "This heavie Act, with heavie heart relate".
Whoever speaks, the words are Othello's.

This accounts for Iago's many self-explanations, which have puzzled
critics, for they seem contrary to his nature, and it is thought that
the man has to be explained on naturalistic grounds. When we
realize that the words are put into his mouth by Othello, and that
his intellectual self-justification is what Othello finds in him, the
difficulty vanishes. Let us look at these speeches. On the principle of
treating the first scene as important we note how fully Iago is made
to state at once what is in his mind, that his ambition is wounded
and how little he loves the Moor, and that he seeks only his own
ends :

> Were I the Moore, I would not be Iago :
> In following him, I follow but myselfe.
> Heaven is my Judge, not I for love and dutie,
> But seeming so, for my peculiar end :
> For when my outward Action doth demonstrate
> The native act, and figure of my heart
> In Complement externe, 'tis not long after
> But I will weare my heart upon my sleeve
> For Dawes to pecke at : I am not what I am.
>
> (1.1)

Nothing could be more explicit than this entire scene:

> Call up her father;
> Rouse him, make after him, poyson his delight,
> Proclaime him in the Streets. Insense her kinsmen,
> And though he in a fertile Clymate dwell,
> Plague him with Flies : though that his Joy be Joy,
> Yet throw such chances of vexation on't,
> As it may lose some colour.

and when the mischief is done:

> Farewell : for I must leave you.
> It seemes not meete, nor wholesome to my place
> To be produced, (as if I stay I shall)
> Against the Moore.

The man does not cease to explain himself, for in the first words of
the next scene he is at it:

> Though in the trade of Warre I have slaine men,
> Yet do I hold it very stuffe o'th' conscience
> To do no contriv'd Murder.   (1.2)

When he resumes talk with Roderigo he declares:

> Virtue? A Figge . . . These Moores are changeable in their wills . . .
> I have told thee often, and I re-tell thee againe and againe, I hate the
> Moore. My cause is hearted; thine hath no sette reason. Let us be
> conjunctive in our revenge, against him. (1.3)

So far we have quoted from speeches to others, but Iago is famous
for self-revealing monologues of which one concludes this scene:

> I hate the Moore,
> And it is thought abroad, that 'twixt my sheets
> He has done my Office. I know not if't be true,
> But I, for mere suspicion of that kinde,
> Will do, as if for Surety.

He lies to himself, to justify himself, and states at once what he
proposes to do to get his revenge, referring to Cassius:

> After some time, to abuse Othello's eares,
> That he is too familiar with his wife:
> He hath a person, and a smooth dispose
> To be suspected: fram'd to make women false.
> The Moore is of a free, and open Nature,
> That thinks men honest, that but seeme to be so,
> And will as tenderly be lead by th' Nose
> As Asses are:
> I have't: it is engendered: Hell, and Night,
> Must bring this monstrous Birth, to the world's light.
>
> (1.3)

Without following these monologues further, we should note how he
is specially self-revealing in his long talks with Roderigo, one of which
takes place in the next act, concluding with a soliloquy in which he
declares his love for Desdemona—

> Not out of absolute lust . . .
> But partly led to dyet my Revenge
> For that I do suspect the lustie Moore
> Hath leap'd into my Seate. The thought whereof,
> Doth (like a poysonous Minerall) gnaw my Inwardes:
> And nothing can, or shall content my Soule
> Til I am even'd with him, wife, for wife.
>
> (2.2)

I have called this Iago's lying to himself; but in this as in the other
speeches Iago's extravagant words are what Othello imaginatively
puts into his mouth, not as the man spoke or thought in fact, for
this is Othello's Iago, as malignant as he can be imagined in thought
as well as deed. For instance the awful act the man is about has to
be set in the vilest light:

> Divinity of hell,
> When devils will the blackest sinnes put on,
> They do suggest at first with heavenly shewes,
> As I do now.
>
> (2.3)

And with the poison well infecting his victim, Iago watches Othello
approach:

> Looke where he comes; Not Poppy, nor Mandragora,
> Nor all the drowsie Syrups of the world
> Shall ever medicine thee to that sweete sleepe
> Which thou owd'st yesterday.
>
> (3.3)

When his villainy is complete his last words are:
> From this time forth, I never will speake word.
>
> (5.2)

I have devoted so much attention to Iago because I am making
the point that the character is here entirely as Othello sees him,
filling his tragic world with overpowering darkness. Desdemona is
the light of life to Othello, but the monster obscures the light. To
discuss Iago as he was in himself, which occupies so much critical
attention, has nothing to do with the drama. His thoughts, his
motives, his career and ambitions, do not concern us at all. These are
matters for history not drama. In the drama, Iago is the sleeping soul of
man; Desdemona the half-awakened soul of woman; Othello acts in the
deep sleep of the instinctive soul until at the climax of the tragedy he
awakens. That is the dramatic action of the play's meaning.

The protagonist's tragic problem is that a man so genuinely in
love should allow himself to be misled so that he destroys what he
most values. Although the action is simple there is complexity, too,
for the hero is a Moor betrayed by Christians, so that the enmity
exceeds that among kindred, and the deepest feelings are aroused.

The Moor is a proud man who knows his worth. At his first appearance he says:

> 'Tis yet to know,
> Which when I know, that boasting is an Honour,
> I shall promulgate. I fetch my life and being,
> From men of Royall Seige. And my demerities
> May speak (unbonnetted) to as proud a Fortune
> As this that I have reach'd.
>
> (1.2)

When he addresses the senate his dignity and self-presence are striking, and the testimony to him by Desdemona is sufficient evidence of his fine quality:

> That I love the Moore, to live with him,
> My downe-right violence, and storme of Fortunes
> May trumpet to the world. My heart's subdu'd
> Even to the very quality of my Lord;
> I saw Othello's visage in his mind,
> And to his Honours and his valiant parts,
> Did I my soule and Fortunes consecrate.
>
> (1.3)

There can be no doubt of the tenderness of the feeling between them. That he should be made to doubt her is utterly incredible: her sins were the "loves she bore" Othello.

At the climax in the last act, when Othello kills his wife as a sacred duty, and at once afterwards sees how he has been misled and the truth appears, he stands in illumination:

> Heere is my journies end, heere is my butt
> And verie Sea-marke of my utmost Saile . . .
> Now—how dost thou looke now? O ill-Starr'd wench,
> Pale as thy Smocke: when we shall meet at compt,
> This look of thine will hurle my Soule from Heaven,
> And Fiends will snatch at it. Cold, cold, my Girle?
> Even like thy Chastity.
>
> (5.2)

That it is illumination at this final moment his last grand and moving words testify:

> When you shall these unluckie deeds relate,
> Speake of me, as I am. Nothing extenuate,

Nor set downe ought in malice.
Then must you speake,
Of one that lov'd not wisely, but too well :
Of one not easily Jealous, but being wrought,
Perplexed in the extreme : Of one, whose hand
(Like the base Indian) threw a Pearle away
Richer than all his Tribe : Of one whose subdu'd Eyes,
Albeit unused to the melting moode,
Drops teares as fast as the Arabian Trees
Their Medicinable Gumme.

The play has a universal appeal because adult men, called to participate in it by making an audience at its performance, find that they themselves in one degree or another have experience of the betrayal of the best by the worst, and in greater or less degree have been guilty of Othello's sin, so that they must say to themselves, Beware! Othello is great in his tragic end. His greatness is not that of a soldier, outstanding as he is, but of one who is freed from his false self, and in utter debasement and agony discovers the truth. That discovery is the play's climax and glory.

The time sequence in the play has caused discussion. Granville Barker has a long troubled discussion upon it saying, "When it is acted we notice nothing unusual", but "the student needs to know". His conclusion is that the play takes place on a single day, from the consummation of the marriage to the tragic end, morning, midday, afternoon, and night, marked by "morning music, dinner-time, supper-time, and the midnight dark". This is mere rhetorical confession of failure in understanding and is unconvincing and unnecessary. There is no need to ask how many hours, months, or years elapsed between Desdemona's elopement and her end, for no answer is required. All happens at once in Othello's mind. Time has no meaning in his vision of events for drama is timeless.

To arouse the sense of timelessness is an essential aim. The consciousness of the spectator is to be freed from the world and natural life to enter into a new realm of experience. This is the great contribution of drama. By its nature poetry effects this detachment, so does music and painting, but in drama it becomes human experience, for the detachment is concretized, made visible, audible and manifest.

THE TRAGEDY OF MACBETH (1606)

In this play the action in natural time is spread over more than eighteen years so that there can be no doubt that we are not witnessing events as they occurred. Moreover, the witches, the ghost of Banquo and the apparitions that appear to Macbeth, suggest that the tests of natural life are not to be applied. The play is on a different level from that of history, and though there was a real Macbeth who became King of Scotland, who had a wife name Gruoch, granddaughter of a king, and there was a King Duncan, his first-cousin, who was killed—in fight, however, not murdered—the play is not concerned with them, but is a poetic creation, a mystery; in short, a vision of the heart of man.

"The whole adjustment of politics to life comes in Macbeth," says Dr. Tillyard in a sentence that conveys the theme of the play, which concerns the political man. Macbeth is a soldier who becomes a politician and a king, and a successful one; the play reveals the state of mind of politicians who stick at nothing to gain their ends. Macbeth's ends are personal: to become king and to maintain himself on the throne; these are a politician's ends, and the intention of Shakespeare, as I read the play, is to show what a politician is— outwardly a success, proud, powerful, and admired, inwardly afflicted with the consequence of the crimes that have brought him to success and his great place. To interpret the play as merely a murder and its consequences, or even as the destructive results of mere ambition, is to undervalue it. There is murder, more than one, and ambition is the motive, but the kind of ambition is all important; it is political ambition.

A. C. Bradley did not see this, which apart from anything else destroys the value of his two chapters. He regards the play (as usual with him) on the level of personal tragedy, in which "a bold ambitious man of action", driven by ambition, aided by a purposeful wife, and misled by evil spirits, embraces evil and commits horrible murder. He reduces the play to melodrama, because he sees Macbeth, and especially Lady Macbeth, as real people, and discusses them as he would discuss the behaviour of historical characters or people read about in a newspaper.

Technically, as drama, the play is highly interesting. In the first place a secondary character, Lady Macbeth, is given large dimensions, not so dominating as actresses and critics have made out, but enormous. When Mrs. Siddons played the part the critics said that the curtain should fall at the end of the sleep-walking scene, as the play had ended, which is what happened at her farewell performance, when an encore was demanded! No doubt she played her solemn brother off the stage, as other actresses have done with their Macbeths, and, if we are to rely upon the descriptions of her playing by contemporary critics, she excelled in the part by naturalistic means.

Bradley gave the character much more attention than he devoted to Macbeth and concluded:

> However appalling she may be, she is sublime.

"*She* almost fades out," complains Quiller-Couch, as, indeed, she does, as the play proceeds, for she ceases to be necessary to the dramatic action. She has nothing to do with the other two murders, and nothing at all to do, except for the sleep-walking, after Banquo's ghost appears, for she has fulfilled her place in Macbeth's vision. To speak of her as "sublime", as Bradley does, is surely to misuse words, though as Macbeth views her in retrospect she is lifted above the ordinary and exalted by wickedness. She is wholly woman, which some critics have interpreted as wholly evil. Certainly, the feminine influence upon Macbeth is evil as he sees it, and as the dramatist, therefore, wishes it to be understood. She provokes the strength of will that drives him to his first murder, and it is profound truth that the darkness of women unillumined by the spirit of man is evil. When the messenger tells her of Duncan's visit, she is transformed:

> Come you Spirits,
> That tend on mortall thoughts, unsex me here,
> And fill me from the Crowne to the Toe, top-full
> Of direst Crueltie: make thick my blood ...
> Come to my Womans Brests,
> And take my Milke for Gall, you muth'ring Ministers ...
> Come thick Night ... (1.4)

That the real woman said anything of the kind we need not suppose. The words put into her mouth are Macbeth's.

The excessive praise of Lady Macbeth as a character in herself is due to the failure to realize that the play is not in any sense whatever her tragedy, large as she is. Nothing but editorial failure to recognize the nature of tragedy, or bad stage production, can depose

Macbeth from his position as protagonist or from making the play his. Lady Macbeth exists only in her relation to him. Whether she was in fact as important an element in the events leading up to Duncan's murder as Macbeth suggests we do not know, nor need we inquire. To him, in vision, hers was the will that drove him on. To discuss Lady Macbeth in any other terms than those of Macbeth is to do violence to the drama. And to see the tragedy, as does Mr. Eliot, as "the weariness of a weak man who had been forced by his wife to realize his own half-hearted desires", is to misjudge the entire work in which she and all the characters take their places in the events that constitute the protagonist's vision; dramatic characterization is concerned with action in drama. Furthermore, at the moment of the play Macbeth was at the height of his powers as Shakespeare takes pains to show, a valiant and victorious soldier: we are meant to admire him. He was, indeed, a hero, and Professor A. C. Sprague (*Shakespeare and the Actors*, 1944) is right when he says, "Macbeth . . . was never, I think, before Irving's time a craven". To present him so is to misjudge the elements of greatness.

The drama is Macbeth's and only his, and unless attention is concentrated upon his acts, aims, state of mind, illumination and death, the play misses its mark, and participation is imperfect. "The theatre of the essential struggle is Macbeth's mind" as a recent American critic says (Donald A. Stauffer, *Shakespeare's World of Images*, New York, 1949). When the play is so understood its meaning is intensified, more profound, more shattering, more poetic, and more exhilarating, than when subjected to naturalistic interpretation.

Among the perplexing features of the play are the three witches, who act as a kind of chorus, and are sometimes supposed to be supernatural: they are natural women enlarged into figures of destiny in Macbeth's imagination. There are, indeed, supernatural beings: Hecat (the spirit of Evil), the ghost of Banquo, the apparitions and the show of eight kings, but they do not include the witches themselves, who are mortal. The supernatural elements bodied forth on the stage are creations of Macbeth's imagination, but so we must reflect are all the characters, and even, as he exists in the play, Macbeth himself. From start to finish the action is concentrated into a single instant. At the opening the words are:

> When the Hurley-burley's done,
> When the Battaile's lost, and wonne.

                                        (1.1)

The end is in the beginning, and the beginning announces the end. "Thunder and Lightning. Enter three Witches" is the first stage direction, and this, I suggest, is how Macbeth sees the drama open. All arises in his mind after the catastrophe as he views what led him to his political success and moral and spiritual downfall. The "brave Macbeth" that "valiant Cousin, worthy Gentleman", was lost in the "fogge and filthie aire". This "fogge" is the atmosphere the dramatist through the protagonist of his play wishes to create. Macbeth declares in his first words, "So foule and faire a day I have not seene," and the words put into the mouths of the witches are his:

> I'le dreyne him drie as Hay :
> Sleepe shall neyther Night nor Day
> Hang upon his pent-house Lid :
> He shall live a man forbid . . .
> Though his Barke cannot be lost,
> Yet it shall be Tempest-tost.
>
> (1.1)

One of the problems of the play never satisfactorily solved is, who was the third murderer in the brief third scene of the third act? The question is treated as unimportant by most critics, but as I think it to be a major question in its bearing upon the theme of this book I invite attention to it.

For this purpose, it is necessary to start with the opening of the third act when Banquo enters alone saying, "Thou hast it now King, Cawdor, Glamis, all, As the weyard Women promis'd", and then goes on to express doubts about Macbeth. The latter enters with his lady and lords and greets Banquo heartily with "Heere's our Chief Guest", requesting his presence at a "solemn Supper" that night. When Banquo accepts, as he must, Macbeth asks casually "Ride you this afternoon?" and is told "Ay, my good Lord". Then "Is't far you ride?" to which Banquo replies that he intends to fill up the time till supper. Follows a third question, "Goes Fleance with you?" which receives the same reply, "Ay, my good Lord". So Banquo goes for his ride, and Macbeth dismisses everyone, telling his servant to bring "those men". Alone, Macbeth discloses himself concerning Banquo :

> To be thus, is nothing, but to be safely thus :
> Our feares in Banquo sticke deepe . . .
>   There is none but he,

> Whose being I doe feare : and under him
> My Genius is rebuk'd, as it is said
> Mark Anthonies was by Caesar.
>
> (3.1)

There is no doubt of his hatred for this one-time friend. He recalls how "the Sisters" prophesied that no son of his would succeed him, and how they hailed Banquo as "Father to a Line of Kings". This he will not endure:

> Rather then so, come Fate into the Lyst,
> And champion me to th' utterance.

The servant returns with "two Murtherers", and then exits. These men, usually ghastly black-wigged creatures, are not, however, professional murderers, but as it appears merely men with a grievance, for Macbeth goes over an earlier conversation and how the grievance they had had against him really applies to Banquo:

> . . . whose heavie hand
> Hath bow'd you to the Grave, and beggar'd
> Yours for ever.

"Soe you," he demands, ". . . finde your patience so predominant . . . that you can let this goe?" Their answer is, "We are men, my Liege". Macbeth works on their ill-nature; both declare they are reckless about what they do; he says plainly that Banquo is as much his enemy as theirs; finally the order to kill the loathed Banquo and his son that night is given and accepted. The murderers are dismissed and Macbeth going off with them says he will call upon them straight.

Then we see Macbeth's Lady and hear that Banquo has gone for his ride, on which Macbeth quickly returns and she shews herself concerned about his uneasy state of mind. "What's done, is done," she urgently says to him, her mind upon the past, but he goes on as though she is not there:

> We have scorch'd the Snake, not killed it . . .
> But let the frame of things disjoint,
> Both the Worlds suffer,
> Ere we will eate our Meale in feare, and sleep
> In the affliction of these terrible Dreames
> That shake us Nightly.
>
> (3.2)

Lady Macbeth does not tolerate such ill-humour and bids him be "bright and Joviall" among his guests; but Macbeth, full of what he is plotting against Banquo, of which he tells her nothing, says to her:

> Let your remembrance apply to Banquo,
> Present him, Eminence, both with Eye and Tongue:

and breaks off, as the colon in the text indicates, to his own problem, that of keeping a successful face upon his uneasy heart:

> Unsafe the while, that wee must lave
> Our Honors in their flattering streames,
> And make our Faces Vizards to our Hearts,
> Disguising what they are.

Then he turns to her, bidding her be jocund, for before the night ends "There shall be done a deed of dreadful note", of which she must be innocent until she applauds the deed, and he ends:

> Come, seeling Night,
> Skarfe up the tender Eye of pittifull Day,
> And with thy bloodie and invisible Hand
> Cancell and tear to pieces that great Bond,
> Which keeps me pale. Light thickens,
> And the Crowe makes Wing to th' Rookie Wood:
> Good things of Day begin to droope, and drowse,
> Whiles Night's black Agents to their Preys doe rowse.
> Thou marvell'st at my words: but hold thee still,
> Things bad begun, make strong themselves by ill:
> So prythee goe with me.

So we arrive at the scene (3.3) to which the preceding has been the ominous preparation. The stage direction is *"Enter Three Murtherers"*. But there had been no more than two attending on Macbeth, and these two are as much astonished as the audience should be at the presence of the third. "But who did bid thee joyne with us?" demands the First Murderer. The answer is "Macbeth". The Second Murderer does not like the presence of the Third, and says so, but the First, ignoring the objection, says, "Then stand with us". Before probing into the question, Who can this Third Murderer be? let us note what happens in this brief but crucial scene of thirty-three lines. The Third Murderer hears the approach of the two for whom they are waiting, "Hearke, I heare Horses". Then the voice of Banquo is heard calling for a light, and the Third Murderer explains that it is usual to walk from that point to the Palace Gate. Banquo and Fleance enter with a torch, and the Third Murderer says, " 'Tis he". Then Banquo recognizes treachery but is struck down, by whom the text does not say, but apparently by the First Murderer as he says, "Let it come downe". The Third cries out, "Who did strike out the Light?" and continues "There's but one downe: the Sonne is fled", for in the darkness Fleance had run off. The Second Murderer saying, "We have lost But halfe of our Affaire", the body of Banquo is dragged away, and the First Murderer declares they will report how much is done. Thus the scene of darkness ends, followed immediately by the bright banquet with Macbeth jocundly welcoming his guests. To this banquet Banquo had been invited.

Now let us ask, Who was the Third Murderer? a question usually brushed aside as unanswerable. A. P. Paton first suggested in April, 1869 (*Notes and Queries*) that he was Macbeth, and gave naturalistic reasons to support the idea. The American H. N. Hudson agreed with him (*Shakespeare His Life, Art and Character*, 1872), but the suggestion was regarded as without foundation, for, it was pointed out, soon after the opening of the Banquet scene, when the First Murderer comes to report to Macbeth, the latter shows concern at Fleance's escape, and when the ghost of Banquo appears, Macbeth cries

> Thou canst not say I did it: never shake
> Thy goary lockes at me.

> (3.4)

These points were regarded as conclusively answering Paton. Moreover it was urged, "How could Macbeth have got away from his lady to join the murderers and return in time to open the banquet?" In his own naturalistic terms Paton was thus disposed of.

Sir Henry Irving in an article in the *Nineteenth Century* (April, 1877) declared that the Third Murderer was the servant who had brought on the two murderers in the first scene. Furness in the Variorum Shakespeare added that the servant must obviously be assumed to be trusty, and he agreed with Irving that he had been sent by Macbeth to see that the two hired men did the job properly. Another critic, M. F. Libby, in 1893, contended that the Third Murderer was Ross. John Masefield in his little book A *Macbeth Production* (1945) said that the Third Murderer "need not puzzle you", and thinks there may have been three to start with, because it could not be expected that two could make a good job of two armed men even in a surprise attack at night. He overlooks the fact that the two murderers were themselves puzzled. Dr. Dover Wilson in *The New Shakespeare*, says that possibly the Third Murderer was originally in the text of the first scene, if not, Shakespeare added him "to show that Macbeth, tyrant-like, feels he must spy even upon his chosen instruments". Sir E. K. Chambers re-introduces doubt by saying, "Are we not to find a supernatural agent in that third murderer?" (*Shakespeare: A Survey*, 1947). Another critic, Roy Walker, in *The Time is Free* (1949) makes this notion of Chambers explicit by suggesting that "the third murderer is the dramatic personification of Macbeth's guilt". George Moore, after being confused by a performance of the play in which there were twenty-two curtains, attempted to show that the whole play had been murdered and suggested that the entire scene was the interpolated work of "some hack who was told to give the public a mixture of mud and blood of melodrama", for Shakespeare was content for the murder to be done off. There was thus, he contends, a Fourth Murderer— the one who botched the play ! (*Conversations with George Moore*, (1929) p. 77).

Let us go back for a moment to the earlier scene where Macbeth is talking to the murderers; it is obvious that this cannot possibly be a record of what took place. Could Macbeth have said in reply to the First Murderer's remark, "We are men, my Liege," what we hear?

> I, in the Catalogue ye goe for men,
> As Hounds, and Greyhounds, Mongrels, Spaniels, Curres,
> Showghes, Water-Rugs, and Demi-Wolves are clept
> All by the Name of Dogges : the valued file
> Distinguishes the swift, the slow, the subtle,
> The House-keeper, the Hunter, every one
> According to the gift, which bounteous Nature
> Hath in him clos'd : whereby he does receive
> Particular addition, from the Bill
> That writes them all alike : and so of men.

> (3.1)

As Macbeth's object was to persuade them to do him a dreadful service one cannot suppose he should have turned upon them so savagely. Of course he did not. What we have in the play is how he looked upon the event at the end, when all was over, when he was denouncing himself. Note that Macbeth enters very closely into what was to be done:

> I will advise you where to plant yourselves,
> Acquaint you with the perfect Spy o' th' time,
> The moment on't . . .

He almost says, "I will be there," and when the murder takes place, Macbeth is there in imagination. In the dramatic vision he sees himself there, though, of course, he was not; in thought he was there, and in mind he followed all that took place; and as the drama is not concerned with actual events but with Macbeth's re-creation of experience in imagination he sees himself directing the murder, and is so involved that it is not easy to say that he did not do it himself. As in the play we are concerned, I say, not with the events but with the drama, we actually see the Third Murderer, and he is Macbeth. That is my solution of the problem.

It will be argued against me that as Macbeth appears in the following scene taking part in the banquet, what time had he to rush away from the murder, and clean and dress himself for the banquet? Shakespeare is never so careless as to involve an actor in such a difficulty, but the question needs only to be asked for its irrelevance to be apparent. If the play is not a record of natural happenings but a work of imagination, the question cannot arise. In imagination everything is simultaneous. In practice on the stage there is sufficient time for the actor to get into the following scene, as Shakespeare well knew. But, it will further be asked, does not Macbeth declare with terror when he sees the bloodstained ghost, "Thou cans't not say I did it"? This terrified exclamation is generally interpreted to mean that while Macbeth did kill Duncan, he had taken care not to kill Banquo, and, indeed, in a physical sense he had not done so, which is what he is declaring. Furthermore, it may be urged that when the First Murderer had reported to Macbeth what had happened, Macbeth appears surprised that Fleance has escaped although the Third Murderer knew it. To be bothered by these matters is to confuse drama with life: of course Macbeth did not know at the time, but in the drama we are concerned with the image, not with reality. Listen to Macbeth's lines, which could not have been the real Macbeth's words for they are a too perfect disclosure of his mind:

Then comes my Fit againe:
I had else beene perfect,
Whole as the Marble, founded as the Rocke,
As broad, and generall, as the casing Ayre:
But now I am cabin'd, crib'd, confin'd, bound in
To saucy doubts, and feares.

(3.4)

These are the visionary Macbeth's words—that is to say the words
of drama. From the naturalistic standpoint what J. Middleton Murray
says of Macbeth's lines generally applies:

> They overcharge the play, and are too powerful for the character or
> the situation to bear; they do not contain the mood or the thought or
> the vision of thwarted ambition or detected murder; they do not
> belong to Macbeth . . .

This disposes of the drama were we to admit the validity of what the
critic says; but as the words do not belong to a natural Macbeth in
a situation that actually occurred but to a dramatic Macbeth, to a
man whose being is in the poetic imagination, the critic is merely
foolish. Unless we understand the play as vision it cannot be understood at all, for as a narration of events it will not stand examination.
This is a perfect drama because the function of the protagonist
is completely fulfilled: he sees himself and his situation in utter
clarity, and invites the spectator to share the experience. A. C.
Bradley wrote of Macbeth:

> What appals him is always the image of his own guilty heart or
> bloody deed, or some image which derives from them its tenor of gloom.
> These, when they arise, hold him spell-bound and possess him wholly,
> like a hypnotic trance which is at the same time the ecstasy of a poet.

Macbeth admits us into his mind without reserve, and his secret
is no secret to us, so that there is nothing to guess at. Thus the play
is drama of the essential kind. All the other characters face towards
Macbeth, and he himself faces towards himself, towards the vision,
which is himself in his inner-most core. Here we have the great
contradiction of drama, which is presented by living actors by whom
we get appearances and spectacle, yet what the dramatist is concerned
with is the inner man. All this is exhibited in the transparent
imagery of Macbeth.
Macbeth is a short play, and many authorities consider the text
to be unsatisfactory; an "abridgment", says Sir E. K. Chambers. A

reason for this is that after the third Act the plot is supposed to go to pieces. The play is thought to be much hacked about, "all broken into little scenes", complained Masefield, and A. C. Bradley was induced to say "The first half of *Macbeth* is greater than the second". I see nothing of the kind, and take exactly the opposite view. The first part is plot, comparatively straightforward and easy for both reader and actor; the second is imaginative creation on the highest level of mental and emotional energy, and extremely difficult, even next to impossible, for reader and actor alike. I find nothing wrong with the text, not even with Hecat and the so-called Middleton bits, including the song, which seems to me essential. Indeed, both Middleton's *The Witch* (1608) and Ben Jonson's *Masque of Queen's* (1609) the more likely borrowed something from Shakespeare, and I am with W. J. Lawrence here (*Shakespeare's Workshop*, 1928).

All actors want to play Macbeth, and almost all fail, often miserably, the reason being that the perfection of the play appeals to them, but their failure is due to their not being equal to the demands of the second part. They can tackle the weird sisters and Lady Macbeth after a fashion, speak the "Is this a dagger" speech, and murder Duncan, kill Banquo, and even encounter his ghost, but there they stop. The apparitions leave them merely perplexed, they are hardly changed by the determination to kill Macduff's wife and babes, which is the play's turning point, Macbeth's fatal error, and when they come to the fifth Act, they are undone:

> I have lived long enough, my way of life
> Is falne into the Seare, the yellow Leafe,
> And that which should accompany Old Age,
> As Honour, Love, Obedience, Troopes of Friends,
> I must not look to have : but in their stead,
> Curses, not lowd but deepe, Mouth-honour, breath
> Which the poore heart would fain deny, and dare not.
>
> (5.3)

What follows, the actor usually carries out as a defeated man, a criminal at bay, which is entirely wrong, for having faced his end Macbeth in the light of that acceptance is able to accept everything, his spirit rising ever higher as his fortunes fall. He is purified, though at a price that should terrify earthly politicians:

> I' ginne to be a-weary of the Sun,
> And wish th' estate o' th' world were now undone.
>
> (5.5)

That his spirit is high and unconquered is declared in his last most
famous words:

> Lay on Macduffe,
> And damn'd be him, that first cries hold, enough.
>   (5.6)

Thus there is called for from the actor the utmost energy, exaltation,
and elevation of body and mind in command of speech and movement. None but the finest and most powerful art is equal to this.
For these reasons the play is practically never seen upon the stage
in its real values, and nearly all editorial commentary seems to me
beside the mark, for unless the nature of drama is realized the true
quality of this great work eludes understanding. It is the test play
for Shakespeare scholarship as it is for Shakespeare stage production.

Macbeth is not a play over which to sentimentalize. We are meant
to look upon Macbeth with the horror with which he contemplates
himself. What redeems the hero is that he faces himself in all his
horror. James I's was a bloody age, much more was Macbeth's.
Murders were in the ordinary course of political action of the time;
none the less, they were morally challengeable, which is what the
play is concerned with. That it is impossible to outwit the judgement
of heaven upon moral fault is the play's theme, Macbeth's fault
being the fundamental fault of egotism, which corrupted the valiant
soldier. Macbeth overcame corruption in his death (which Lady
Macbeth did not) which makes the tragic drama. "The time is free",
declares Macduff at the end, bringing in the bloody head. We should
understand these to be the dead Macbeth's words.

I do no more than touch upon the wonders of this play, for I am
concerned only to indicate how the law of drama is observed in what
is possibly the greatest dramatic work in any language.

THE TRAGEDY OF KING LEAR (1606)

To say that any one play is the greatest work of Shakespeare is
not profitable, for there is not a single greatness, but many glories.
The play to which we have now come, is, Professor G. Wilson
Knight says, "life's abundance magnificently compressed into one
play". A recent expositor, Mr. John F. Danby, says of it:

> Shakespearean drama is literally a new organ of thought. It is only

dramatically that the manner of living thought can be adequately expressed.

That drama does what no other literary work and no other art can do is part of my purpose in this book to establish. In Shakespeare, dramatic art reached its highest achievement, and his plays are in a different category from those of other Elizabethan dramatists, being works of true drama, while most of the plays of his time, not all, and most plays written since, though not all, are little more than theatrical entertainments. The content of Shakespeare's plays makes them supreme among the works of man.

This supremacy is illustrated by *King Lear*, the most human as well as the most comprehensive of the plays. Though he made use of an earlier play, the *True Chronicle History of King Leir* and Holinshed's *Chronicles*, Shakespeare created a new thing. To check what he was doing or to interpret what he did by reference to the *Chronicles* or the earlier play is, however, a grave mistake. In the original *Leir*, the division of the kingdom had not taken place before the play starts, and Lear's rage with Cordelia does not appear until late in the third scene, and there are other differences; there is no need to suppose that light can be thrown upon Shakespeare's work by examining its sources.

What Shakespeare set out to do was to create in Lear a protagonist able to invite an audience to participate in the complete abandonment of the human heart to suffering. Such a protagonist had to be strong, noble, high minded, and in a high place, yet brought so low that pity is exhausted by weakness, folly, misery and death. What Shakespeare does through this character is to enable the spectator to enter into the uttermost depths of human loss and to rejoice in the victory of the human spirit. The play is Lear's vision. Everything essential to dramatic action is contained in it, the vision is complete. Neither time nor place are of consequence, nor the events of nature, nor the histories of the characters, or what they were in themselves. All that matters is the vivid, startling, heart-breaking, yet exhilarating vision; and to enter into it so that its images become the spectator's own, so that he sees displayed his own life, and can experience in imagination what he may be saved from in life, are the dramatist's aims.

To regard the play as the story of an actual man as A. C. Bradley does in his two chapters and to judge it in the terms of natural life

is to be led astray, as I think is the fate of Bradley and all who
follow him. Bradley thinks the play to be the greatest of Shakespeare's
works, but points out that it is the least popular, the least acted, and
the least successful of the four great tragedies! The reason is, he
thinks, that "strictly as drama", it is inferior to the other three, it is
"imperfectly dramatic" and "demands a purely imaginative realiza-
tion", which is a strange conclusion to a judgement that has placed
the play so high and a positive indication of Bradley's lack of
understanding of drama. Shelley said of the play:

> King Lear . . . may be judged to be the most perfect specimen of the
> dramatic art in the world; in spite of the narrow conditions to which
> the poet was subjected by the ignorance of the philosophy of drama
> that has prevailed in modern Europe.

There are critics who find in it the "despairing depths of voiceless
and inexplicable agony" (Addington Symonds), but being a play it
has a voice, and being a tragic drama it is not despairing. On the
contrary its language is exalted and the spectator is brought to
exquisite delight. Only those who look for rationality in the
characters are horrified and think it to be "defective drama". Bradley
sets out in detail what he considers to be wrong with it as a play,
but I do not propose to enter into the discussion, for Harley Granville
Barker has dealt with him in his own courteous and gentle manner.
Barker was, however, it seems to me over-awed by Bradley's vast
learning, and followed him too closely in his elaborate consideration
of the play. What Barker says of Shakespeare is to the point, however:

> . . . his admitted task was to make his play stageworthy. In his greatest
> drama we should at least look for his greatest stagecraft.

That, in Barker's view, is what we find, which must be the view of
all who have approached the play rightly. What Shakespeare set
out to do he carried out successfully. The greatness of the work is
in its greatness as drama, which includes stageworthiness.

Certainly the play presents difficulties in what it demands of
producers and actors and in particular of the leading actor. Lear is
more than life-size and cannot be brought within the dimensions of
natural man, however large and powerful. The character belongs to
the imagination, a realm in which actors should know how to move.
As a practical dramatist who understood the stage for which he was
writing, Shakespeare must have considered that the part could be

F

performed so as to fulfil his dramatic object. Yet one wonders whether Shakespeare was satisfied with Burbage, or whether he could have anticipated Shaw in the declaration that he, Shakespeare, was "the only person in the theatre who knew that the whole affair was a ghastly failure". Burbage, however, appears to have been a man of imagination.

In our day and for more than two hundred years past failure with the play has always initially been due to misinterpretation, which is why, as George Gordon remarked, Paris hated it when performed there about 1920, "regarding it as stupid and idiotic". Were those responsible for its staging and acting to ignore not only its stage history but also the commentators and instead give intensive study to the text, realizing the dramatic action with confidence in the dramatist, they would discover its acting possibilities. Otherwise they cannot meet its profound demands, so that we get the performances to which we are used, which put discriminating audiences into two minds about the play even when they are disposed to admire the leading actor, and finally everyone is led to Charles Lamb's conclusion that "*Lear* is essentially impossible to be represented on the stage". I confess that I have never seen an actor not overcome by the part, emitting distressing signs of the fact that he cannot cope with it because he struggles with a misconceived task. Were he to treat the character including the events of nature within it as dramatic action in vision, it would be brought within the range of art.

Lamb saw only Nathan Tate's version, under the conditions of the picture stage. Coming from such a performance he could do no less than write:

> On the stage we see nothing but corporal infirmities and weakness, the impotence of rage; while we read it, we see not Lear, but we are Lear,—we are in his mind, we are sustained by a grandeur which baffles the malice of daughters and storms.

This is proof of the actor's failure: for the play was not written to be read but to be seen, with a corporeal Lear, and to condemn the dramatist for the actor's deficiencies is unjust. Leigh Hunt had different grounds for agreeing that the play should not be performed:

> An actor who performs Lear truly, should so terrify and shake the town, as to be requested never to perform the part again.

But Hunt was thinking of "a mad old father in the public street", that is to say he expected realistic playing. Yet, in truth, were *Lear* played as its creator intended, the town would shake, and no one who participated would remain as he was before, because the play is a transforming experience. What one of the popular American Commentators (Stoll) says of one of the scenes that it is "stylized" or, as he prefers "unrealistic", "even at the characters' expense", I say applies to the entire play; for it contains not two techniques but one, the technique of poetic drama. Critics who do not know what that is should not be critics of Shakespeare.

Throughout, the structure of the play is masterly. In the opening scene, after a few introductory speeches of importance, Lear comes on immediately and the audience is plunged into the heart of the tragedy. Granville Barker said that the play's greatness was in its verse, meaning in what the verse does. For the action in the terms of poetic imagery contains Lear's problem, which is opened in this first scene: how to overcome the results of folly and self-will, folly in dividing his kingdom and still wishing to be king, and in not knowing the true nature of his two elder daughters; self-will in disinheriting Cordelia and failing to recognize her virtue. In self-will, Lear divests himself, with his kingdom, of everything, except what he has from God, his kingship, and from nature, his age, to both of which he clings. Thus he strips himself of his worldly senses, keeping to represent them only the Fool, who is unable to protect him; so that he is left exposed to the evils that descend upon un-accommodated man, "a poor, bare, fork'd animal".

The play plunges Lear immediately into the action when he demonstrates his folly, demanding that his daughters should say which "doth love us most". The two elder do not spare their flattering words, but the youngest will not speak, not pandering to her father's weakness. Cordelia, agreed to be one of Shakespeare's most appealing woman characters, has perplexed almost everyone by her silence. She appears out of place on any naturalistic interpretation, for who can have patience with the (supposedly) peevish girl! But she is as Lear sees her with opened eyes at the end, not as she was at the time; in such a situation silence only was appropriate to the presence of goodness incarnated. She exists in this scene as an angel, and should be looked upon (and played) in the terms of the last act when Lear is weeping over her dead body. To think of her in these terms is to realize how marvellous she is, the scene becomes illuminated and what is regarded as a tiresome opening shines in brilliance.

With the coming up of the dark cloud of the bastard Edmund in the second scene, the complication of Gloucester and his two sons is set going to increase dramatic complexity and to prevent the action from becoming obvious, otherwise there is no need for the so-called underplot. All, however, is related to Lear and belongs to his tragedy. Gloucester is involved by Lear in Lear's fate, and that he should be broken is part of Lear's burden. Those who complain that Shakespeare was "pandering to base appetites", in the looseness of Edmund's behaviour, also when Gloucester's eyes were put out and he wanders blind, do not realize how Shakespeare was bringing the audience into the depths of Lear's agony.

His suffering becomes cosmic when the heavens thunder, and the mad Lear cries:

> Blow windes, and crack your cheeks; Rage, blow
> You Cataracts, and Hytricano's spout,
> Till you have drench'd our Steeples, drown the Cockes.
> You Sulph'rous and Thought-executing Fires,
> Vaunt-Curriors of Oake-cleaving Thunder-bolts,
> Sindge my white head. And thou all-shaking Thunder,
> Strike flat the thicke Rotundity o' th' world,
> Cracke Natures moulds, all germaines spill at once
> That makes ungratefull Man.

(3.2)

In these words Lear neither competes with Nature nor cowers under the storm. George Gordon referred to *Lear* as "a convulsion of Nature", as "a great natural upheaval", but the convulsion is not Nature's, it is that of the human heart. Lear is defying Nature, proving himself to be above Nature. What Lamb so profoundly said should be recalled here:

> The greatness of Lear is not in corporal dimensions, but in intellectual; the explosions of his passion are terrible as a volcano,—they are storms turning up and disclosing to the bottom of the sea, his mind, with all its vast riches. It is his mind which is laid bare.

The key words are "intellectual", and "his mind", for the storm is Lear's own creation. The storm is in his mind, in his tempestuous, outraged thoughts, so that he becomes responsible for the thunders and winds of the world that beat upon him. The scene displays the height of Lear's stature. On the stage, the storm is required to be in the art of the actor not in the mechanics of the effects man; unless it is apparent that the storm is the affair of this enormous spiritual mountain of a king, the scene has not been played. To drown Lear's words in thunder so that the actor cannot be heard is theatrical nonsense. Not long after the storm the Fool disappears, for worldly wits are no more active in the play—"Ile go to bed at noone", he says, and passes away. The Fool is not intended to be sentimentalized, a fact almost invariably forgotten.

One of the problems is Edgar, at first a mild young man of the court who becomes Old Tom, falsely banished, pretending madness, pretending to lead his blinded father to the cliffs of Dover to destroy himself, pretending to be a peasant, finally the instrument of justice and reconciliation. He is not to be explained on his own terms, but as a figure in the protagonist's vision of charity. He exists only in vision, realized in one of the strangest scenes in the play where he, his demented father, and the mad Lear meet.

Without discussing characters and action further I say no more than that this tightly compressed play is at its dramatic best in the last scene where at the opening the enprisoned Lear says softly to Cordelia :

> come let's away to prison,
> We two alone will sing like Birds i' th' Cage :
> When thou dost aske me blessing, Ile kneele downe
> And aske of thee forgivenesse : So wee'l live
> And pray, and sing, and tell old tales, and laugh
> As gilded Butterflies ...
> And take upon's the mystery of things ...
>
> (5.3)

He finds himself blessed in nothingness and the play ends quickly after Lear's :

> ... no, no, no life?
> Why should a Dog, a Horse, a Rat have life,
> And thou no breath at all ? Thou'lt come no more,
> Never, never, never, never, never.
>
> (5.3)

In intense pathos the uttermost sorrow is lifted up until it becomes exaltation, echoed in the last words of the play spoken by Edgar :

> ... we that are young,
> Shall never see so much, nor live so long.

Professor Una Ellis-Fermor argues in *The Frontiers of Drama* (1945) that the purification in tragedy is in the balance of opposing forces. She considers that Aeschylus presents evil in the actions and words of the characters and good in the words of the Chorus, while she offers Cordelia and Kent as examples of the opposites of the evil characters in *Lear*, so that the spectator at the play is enabled to maintain equilibrium between two ideas. On the contrary, I suggest that the purification is specifically in the crisis of the dramatic action, when Lear himself is purified. In that crisis, not in anything concerning the other characters, is contained the equilibrium, which she rightly says is what follows from the evil being accepted.

An American critic has found fault with Lear because he "self-dramatizes", not perceiving that it is what every protagonist does. This play is as great as it is because the protagonist is fully realized, because his problem is one into which every audience can enter, and because the whole and the conclusion to which the action is brought become a poetic vision of the most intense kind.

THE TRAGEDY OF ANTHONY AND CLEOPATRA (1607)

This is a play suffused with splendour. From start to finish it is at the height of passionate exaltation set in the midst of the vast riches of Egypt and never falls below that height except for brief moments. Coleridge wondered whether "in all exhibitions of a giant power in its strength and vigour of maturity" it were not a formidable rival of the four great tragedies. He calls it "by far the most wonderful" and "astonishing". Professor Wilson Knight describes it as the work of "the transcendent erotic imagination". Granville Barker says, "here is the most spacious of the plays . . . it has a magnificence and a magic all its own". It is, in short, a work of genius, and we need not go further among the critics for confirmation.

That it is Anthony's play, he being the protagonist and the vision his, all critics with few exceptions agree. They may attempt the impossible by bringing in Cleopatra as a second protagonist, so vividly is that character impressed upon their minds, and there are even a few who would throw over Anthony and make her the protagonist (as some actresses attempt to do); but all this is mere critical weakness.

It is certainly a drama of action in a special sense, action that extends throughout Egypt and from Egypt to Rome, and above all action in the bursting mind and heart of its protagonist:

> . . . the triple Pillar of the world transformed
> Into a Strumpet's foole.

In the opening scene, after no more than ten lines of introduction, Anthony and Cleopatra appear, and the excess of passion spills over:

> If it be Love indeed, tell me how much.
> Theres beggery in the love that can be reckon'd.
> I'll set a bourne how far to be belov'd.
> Then must thou needes finds out new Heaven, new Earth.

These words "new Heaven, new Earth", are the key words of the play; for this is not Egypt in history or the heaven hoped for by believers, but a heaven and earth made new by passion.

There can be no doubt about Anthony's problem, it is passion. A soldier, man of action, and world politician, he is held by the heart, by the hand of a woman, and ruined. The play is bright, hard, expansive, shining with glory, without a touch of meanness, soaring in spirit, heated with burning emotion, and the hurtling fire of passionate love brings all down to destruction and death. For such passion is death-dealing. It is beautiful, but terrifying; and the first sight of Anthony with Cleopatra on his arm should make every spectator's heart shake.

The music of the verse is without parallel even in Shakespeare, for music is emotion. Says Edith Sitwell:

> . . . the whole play is one of the greatest miracles of sound that has ever come into this world.

Indeed, the play takes one's breath away from moment to moment, so that one sits entranced. It is the verse that makes the play tolerable and in no other play is drama so richly and fully contained in verse, for there are no speeches that exist for their own sake, no rhetorical displays, no soliloquys and few monologues, the verse is concentrated upon the theme. Intensity is the play's supreme element; once that is grasped its difficulties are surmountable so long as nothing is sacrificed to the centrality of Anthony.

An apparent difficulty about Anthony as protagonist is that he dies in the fourth Act, with the result that Cleopatra grows in importance, which leads Granville Barker to say "the domination of the play passes at once to Cleopatra". Without paying attention to the word "domination", one must say that Barker was wrong, for the play remains Anthony's. There is no real difficulty when it is understood that the long drawn-out close has him still as the central figure, though dead. What Bradley said was entirely without foundation that Shakespeare paid Cleopatra "a unique compliment" by devoting the whole of the fifth Act to her: he did nothing of the kind. The play is still about Anthony, for Cleopatra is there only in relation to him. She has to die because he is dead. The fifth Act opens, "Go to him . . .", and the 369 lines of the Act are overshadowed, permeated, by Anthony, they contain his vision, and when Caesar learns that he is dead he says:

> The round World
> Should have shooke . . .
> The death of Anthony
> Is not a single doome, in the name lay
> A moity of the World.
> . . . it is Tydings
> To wash the eyes of Kings.
>
> (5.1)

Testimony to Anthony continues on the highest level in Cleopatra's words:

> My desolation does begin to make
> A better life . . . and it is great
> To do that thing that ends all other deeds
> Which shackles accidents, and bolts up change;
> Which sleepes, and never pallates more the dung,
> The beggers Nurse, and Caesar's.
>
> (5.2)

And when she hears from Caesar, she defies him in death's name but is soon in a rhapsody upon Anthony:

> His face was as the Heav'ns, and therein stucke
> A Sunne and Moone, which kept their course, and lighted
> The little o' th' earth . . .
> His legges bestrid the Ocean, his Rear'd arme
> Crested the world: His voyce was propertied
> As all the tuned Spheres, and that to Friends:
> But when he meant to quaile, and shake the Orbe,

He was as rattling Thunder. For his Bounty,
There was no winter in't. An Anthony it was
That grew the more by reaping: His delights
Were Dolphin-like, they shewed his backe above
The Element they liv'd in: In his Livery
Walk'd Crownes and Crownets: Realms and Islands were
As plates dropt from his pocket . . .
Think you there was, or might be such a man
As this I dreampt of?

                                        (5.2)

The level of the verse continues as she humbles herself to Caesar,
and is not lowered when she learns that he intends her to be in his
Triumph to Rome. Her answer is:

                Go fetch
        My best Attyres. I am againe for Cidrus,
        To meete Marke Anthony . . .
        My Resolution's plac'd, and I have nothing
        Of woman in me: Now from head to foote
        I am Marble constant: now the fleeting Moone
        No Planet is of mine.

Who can but think that the rest of the play, until Caesar utters the
concluding "See High Order, in this great Solemnity", is anything
but Anthony's own vision and his words?

Although they admire the character, the critics have also found
Cleopatra baffling and the character defective. The learned Levin
Ludwig Schueckling points out:

 . . . we never see her acting as a queen at all. Nobody would suspect
 that this woman, as Plutarch informs us, has for years, quite unaided,
 ruled a great kingdom. She never gives audience, never exercises the
 functions of her high office. Love seems to be her only aim in life.

He does not realize that Cleopatra is a female image in Anthony's
mind. What had her functions as a queen to do with this? His
comment does, however, have the effect, I think, of confirming what
I am endeavouring to say.

A study of the other scenes in which Anthony does not appear
would also seem to support the view of the play it is my object to
establish. In no other play is so much said about the protagonist, his
actions and character, as in this. From first to last the play is
Anthony's. All the leading Romans with the exception of Ventidius
appear in an unfavourable light, as they would appear to Anthony:

F*

Caesar as mean, Lepidus weak, Pompey foolish, Enobarbus corrupted, and the Roman people are

> ... our slippery people,
> Whose Love is never link'd to the deserver,
> Till his deserts are past.

(1.2)

It must be admitted, I think, that the real difficulty, grand as the play is, is that we cannot wholly sympathize with Anthony, because of excessive love and great failure as a soldier. Despite its brilliance and fascination, the play is a little displeasing, which perhaps enables us to bear our delight.

THE TRAGEDY OF CORIOLANUS (1607)

This is a play in which a politician cannot reconcile himself to what is required for political success. He is a soldier, none more successful, and the two fields of activity—politics and arms—are contrasted to the disadvantage of the former. The audience is intended to sympathize with the protagonist, Coriolanus, to accept him as noble, able and genuine, and to examine themselves in this matter of politics as they enter into the tragedy. Coriolanus is not, however, held up as blameless; for he is uncontrolled and impulsive, "passion's slave" and therefore disastrously wrong. Middleton Murry thought the theme of the play to be pride, but, while the hero is inordinately proud, the theme, I think, is concerned with what provokes the display of pride in him, the demands of politics.

The hero's faults of self-will, arrogance, and, as we have agreed, pride, will not allow him to accommodate himself to the requirements of political office; these faults bring about his failure and death. It is a play, however, not only for politicians, though especially for them, but also for the populace, for those who make use of politicians: therefore for the audience collaborating in its performance.

Coriolanus has always been regarded as an important play, though it has never been a popular one because the hero though great is not presented in a favourable light. It is a severe play, and on that ground is avoided on the stage. Furthermore, Shakespeare does not flatter the masses. As his hero treats the people with contempt, Shakespeare appears to lean in the same direction. Indeed, the play raises among other questions of political importance how the masses should be handled. Coriolanus was not successful; but there must be a right way, which is not that of deception, a way Coriolanus refuses to take.

The attitude of the critics shows considerable divergence of opinion. Johnson found the play "the most amusing of our author's performances", an extraordinary judgement. Coleridge considered that it "illustrates the wonderfully philosophic impartiality of Shakespeare's politics". Hazlitt thought it "a store-house of political commonplaces". Bradley thought the hero "a lovable being" and the play "noble". T. S. Eliot thinks it Shakespeare's "most perfect work of art"; "Shakespeare's most assured artistic success". Granville Barker considered that it could not be ranked with the greatest of the tragedies.

The key to the play is to be found as always in the opening scene, where the citizens demand the death of the soldier Marcius, afterwards named Coriolanus. They are starving, and he is "a very dog to the Comonalty". It is clear that they grant him merit, though "partly proud", and speak "in hunger for Bread, not in thirst for Revenge". Then appears Menenius, the perfect politician, who, with a parable of the body and its members, pacifies the mob, in the glib manner of politicians, until Marcius enters. He treats them with contempt, "Get you home you Fragments", he says. There is news that "the Volsies are in Armes", so the two go to the senate, and the abashed citizens steal away, while we hear what the tribunes think of Marcius, "Was ever man so proud?"

There is elevation in this scene and the sense of a dangerous situation, war outside and unrest within. Afterwards, Marcius attacks and defeats the enemy, the battle scenes being long and elaborate, for this is a play of spectacle. Marcius appears great in personal combat, and goes on fighting though covered with wounds. He is received in triumph in Rome, named Coriolanus, and offered the Consulship; but he will not submit himself to the people until at last induced to do so, but he behaves in a way to increase enmity against him. As a result of this enmity he is banished from Rome, joins its enemies, and at their head defeats the Romans; but in the moment of triumph, a conspiracy against him causes his death.

No matter the party, the honest man in politics is betrayed.

For our present purposes, there is no need to examine the play in detail because there is no doubt about the central character. What has to be remembered is that he presents the tragedy; what he is

called upon to do, how he does it, and the outcome, are as Coriolanus
sees the events in vision at the end.

THE LIFE OF TIMON OF ATHENS (1607)

All the tragedies are closely related. All have as heroes men deeply
concerned with public affairs. Their problems are personal, but each
is in a situation that is more than personal and the background of
each is political. That is true of this last tragedy, which begins and
ends in a political atmosphere. Yet the tragedy is a personal one,
the protagonist being utterly destroyed, even, he declares, in his soul.
It is an astonishing play, vigorous, violent, and catastrophic in the
highest degree, but over it is a golden light that makes it tolerable:
a bitter tragedy, with a kernel of sweetness. Notable for having no
women characters, except two courtesans, it is wholly masculine,
intellectual at its core, and for that reason not popular. Critics find
in it other hands than Shakespeare's, and are divided between thinking it a play revised by him or a play of his revised by another.
Mostly this criticism is inspired by the desire to treat the plot as
rational and the characters as merely human. As the plot is poetic
drama and the characters imaginary the criticism is beside the mark.

Yet as Hazlitt pointed out, *Timon* is "written with as intense
a feeling of its subject as any one play of Shakespeare". It is Greek
in its economical simplicity of structure, displaying the irreconcil-
ability of earthly and heavenly riches. Commonly, the theme is said
to be ingratitude: Timon's folly in being generous and neglecting
prudence, which turns him against mankind. Ingratitude is a merely
literal interpretation, however, for Timon's rejection by his friends
forecasts his own rejection of the world. The theme is not in what
happens to Timon but in Timon's own act of complete rejection
even of life itself; in that act is also his redemption. Timon's problem
is how to be reconciled with men, a fundamental human problem,
which he solves not in a human but divine way. The play requires
acting of the most intense kind in the principal part.

From our present point of view I have only to emphasize that the
play should be understood as Timon's vision and that the characters,
except Timon, are not to be accepted on their own terms. When it
opens, a poet, printer, jeweller, merchant and mercer meet, after
them come certain senators: the scene is as Timon presents it, this

is Timon's view. When he appears, almost his first words point to his own fate:

> I am not of that Feather, to shake off
> My Friend when he most needs me.
>
> (1.1)

This is his view of himself. The play provides a contrast between the splendour of Timon's life in Athens in the first three Acts, and the wretchedness of his life when he casts himself off from the city in the last two. He is master of wealth and the delight of the world in the first, and equally master of himself and his own hate of the world in the second. In this contrast lies the play's greatness.

The most significant scene is the duologue in the fourth Act between himself and the churlish philosopher, Apemantus, who has nothing but ill to say of the world. Timon in the wood is abandoned to his cave, and is digging for gold, which he finds in the rocks only to treat as worthless. So, too, does the irreconcilable philosopher regard it; but they are not of the same mind. Timon asks him:

> What would'st thou do with the world Apemantus, if it
> lay in thy power?

> Give it to the Beasts, to be rid of the men.

> Would'st thou have thyself fall to the confusion of men,
> and remain a Beast with the Beasts?

> I Timon.

> A beastly Ambition . . .
>
> (4.3)

Though Timon hates men, he does not enter the world of beasts nor is he subject to the beast in himself. That is the solution of his problem.

> My long sicknesse
> Of Health and Living, now begins to mend,
> And nothing brings me all things.

It is a terrible play for all who are attached to earthly things, for Timon overcomes the world by hate that is love in its convulsive aspect. I think the play can be recognized as great drama in that sense, as vision, lifted out of natural life. The "nothing" that brings Timon "all things" is reconciliation and redemption, thus the play is perfect drama.

THE FINAL PERIOD
(1608-1613)

Pericles—Cymbeline—The Winter's Tale—The Tempest—
King Henry VIII.

THESE plays were, perhaps, written at Stratford-on-Avon, when Shakespeare had returned thither, though why he retired we do not know. Perhaps, as Dr. Dover Wilson suggests in his book, *What Happens in Hamlet,* he had some trouble with his company. During the period the company had acquired the Blackfriars Theatre in which plays could be given under rather different conditions from those at the open Globe, and that this might have led to some change in Shakespeare's writing is easy to understand, for the main new features at the new theatre were the increase of intimacy with the audience and possibilities of more elaborate staging. But the new theatre must have given new opportunities to Shakespeare, and the disagreement with his company, which must have been profound, may have been that the actors wanted no more tragedies.

That seems to be indicated in *Pericles,* which is a problem in every sense of the word, and there is doubt as to its being Shakespeare's. If it be his, new elements are indicated in his work, a total departure from the manner of the tragedies, and the law of drama cannot be recognized. Anyhow, Shakespeare did not repeat the experiment. In the succeeding four plays, three tragi-comedies, and a history, the law is clearly observed, even in the last, another problem play, and disputed to be Shakespeare's. These plays indicate the development of a new technique, perhaps also of a new outlook and deepened insight. All are difficult plays, making great demands upon players and the theatre, and equally severe demands are made upon the attention of spectators. Had he not died so early, London might have had a greater Shakespeare, surpassing all that had gone before. To suppose that, in Prospero, Shakespeare was taking leave of his art, as nearly all the editors do, is probably far from the truth.

These final plays are distinguished works, which with the possible exception of the first could have been written by none but the great master of drama.

PERICLES, PRINCE OF TYRE (1608)

This piece was omitted from the First Folio, no doubt for the good reason that it is not on the level of Shakespeare's other works. Possibly he disliked it. It had been published as a Quarto with Shakespeare's name in 1609, and again in the same year, also in 1611, and 1619, so that Shakespeare and his editors were well aware of his being credited with it. None the less it was rejected. These separate publications are evidence of the play's popularity, for it was printed again in 1630, for a sixth time in 1635, and admitted into the Third Folio of 1664 with other plays not by Shakespeare. At the restoration, it was the first Shakespeare play to be performed by the Duke's Company.

Although the most learned critics are now ready to admit it to be at least in part by Shakespeare, it is hard to reconcile the play with his other works. There is a possibility (I do not think so) that it was a very early work, which he re-wrote for his company, clamouring for something easier and more popular than the tragedies. We do not know, and can do no more than guess. A "mouldy tale", says Ben Jonson; and it is certainly a tale, a romance, appealing to the public taste because of spectacle, ample incident, storms and shipwreck, dumb-shows, and some magic.

The play is a dramatic entertainment, a play in form but mere story-telling. It has a hero, Pericles, but he is a story hero, not a hero of drama, as he does not fulfil what is required of a protagonist. Why that is so is worth a brief study.

In his valuable essay on "The Writing of Pericles", in *The Crown of Life* (1947), Professor Wilson Knight discusses the play in detail, and gives reasons for thinking it to be, as a whole, Shakespeare's. He says of the chief character:

> Pericles himself is a passive figure, quite unlike Shakespeare's usual dynamic protagonists. He himself does nothing crucial: his fall is purely an awareness of evil . . . his good acts are perfunctorily set down, his repentance in sackcloth and unshaven hair is a repentance for no guilt of his own but rather for the fact of mortality in a harsh universe. He is here for things to happen to and forges little or nothing for himself.

That seems to dispose of Pericles as a protagonist. The character is touching, and had Shakespeare wished to make his piece drama, no doubt he could have done so; but this he avoided. Pericles cannot invite the audience to participate, he does not present his problem in vision, and he does not give the piece unity. His asides are not self-revelatory but explanatory, and the unity of the piece is in the hands of the chorus, named Gower, who was the poet from whose works Shakespeare took the story.

We see from this piece that a work that has a plot, characters, dialogue, and is intended to be performed on a stage, need not be a drama, though successfully brought off. The play sets out to excite and beguile an audience, which Shakespeare showed that he could do as well as any other, but the result is something different from drama, though using the same instruments. It is much less than drama because it does not invite participation, only observation or perception, and remains superficial. That Shakespeare did not consider this kind of writing worth doing is shown by the fact that he attempted nothing more in this much easier medium, easier for dramatist, actors, and audience. That he was right is shown by the fact that of all Shakespeare's works Pericles has lost even its theatrical value, its one-time popularity having evaporated.

THE TRAGEDY OF CYMBELINE (1610)

This perhaps was the first Shakespeare play written for the Black-friars Theatre. There is no record of its being performed there, however, only a performance at the Globe is noted, but that may not have been the first. It has been among the best loved of the plays and must have been well liked when first performed. David Garrick made the leading character one of his favourite parts. Yet it is a vast and difficult play, highly complicated in its action; the vision is wide-ranging and not readily followed. A. C. Bradley did not class it as a tragedy, in which he was right, for it is tragi-comedy. We should note that Bradley was much upset by what he regarded as the glaring fault of dialogue intended to be spoken openly to the audience.

The first question is, Who is the protagonist? Cymbeline, who gives the play his name, is, though King of Britain, weak and in-decisive, dominated by his Queen, and has none of the features of a protagonist. Imogen, the heroine, his daughter, might be thought of, for she seems to bind the action together, but what the drunken lord says to Cloten has matter in it:

> . . . her Beauty and her Braine go not together.
>
> (1.3)

She is not the one who has a vision. Iachimo, the villain, has a showy part, and though actors sometimes treat him as the lead, he is not the central character. There is left Posthumus, a young man, and though much of the action takes place in his absence and he is rather colourless, needing an actor of colourful personality to fill the part, there can be no doubt that he is the protagonist. That the play is his is pointed to in the opening scene:

> I do not think
> So faire an Outward, and such Stuffe within
> Endows a man, but hee?
>
> (1.1)

He is the presenter and the vision is his. The situations are sharp, vivid, and exaggerated because he is often absent and imagines them. He is banished at the opening, and all that concerns Imogen, whom he has married against the King's will, and the Queen's too, for she wants the Princess for her son, is imagined. Imogen is surrounded by evil, as the absent man fears. The Queen, who is not her mother, seeks to undermine her loyalty to her husband; her son, Cloten, foul in appearance and in mind, tries to seduce her; and Posthumus, having wagered with an Italian gentleman, Iachimo, that he could not overcome her virtue, foolishly adds to the evil.

Posthumus's problem is how to remove the King's objection to him and to be re-united to Imogen; but he creates for himself a new problem by doubts about his wife, believing that Iachimo has succeeded. The unity of the plot is established by his mind being steadily upon Imogen throughout.

The character against whom Posthumus has most reason to feel harshly, the Queen, is presented as a horrible and entirely evil being. She devotes herself to making deadly poisons which she proposes to use, so that she is warned:

> Your Highnesse
> Shall from this practice, but make hard your heart . . .
>
> (1.6)

but "O content thee", is her reply. The physician who aids her has a speech in the same scene, spoken to the audience (this is not the speech Bradley objected to) in which he expresses his dislike, and says he will fool her. In the end she dies, to everyone's relief,

> O most delicate Fiend !
> Who is't can reade a Woman?
> (5.8)

There are many soliloquies intended to be spoken to the audience, evidence of the new stage conditions at the Blackfriars Theatre where there was much greater intimacy than at the Globe, because it was smaller; at the same time it offered better means of elaboration in staging. There can be no doubt that the great speeches in all the plays were delivered directly to the audience, without the actor stepping out of contact with the other players; but in this play there is clear indication that the soliloquies were designed to take advantage of the smaller theatre and to use to the full audience participation. When Posthumus is falsely told by Iachimo that he had won her honour, Posthumus has a long violent speech denouncing women :

> Could I finde out
> The Woman's part in me, for there's no motion
> That tends to vice in man, but I affirme
> It is the Woman's part : be it Lying, note it,
> The womans : Flattering, hers : Deceiving, hers :
> Lust, and ranke thoughts, hers, hers : Revenges, hers :
> Ambitions, Covetings, change of Prides, Disdaine,
> Nice-longing, Slanders, Mutability :
> All Faults that name, nay, that Hell knowes,
> Why hers, in part, or all : but rather all For even to Vice
> They are not constant, but are changing still;
> One Vice, but of a minute old, for one
> Not half so old as that. Ile write against them,
> Detest them, curse them : yet 'tis greater Skill
> In a true Hate, to pray they have their will :
> The very Devils cannot plague them better.

(2.5)

This direct speaking is a feature of the play, and there are many long and short speeches of a similar kind.

Imogen flies to wild Wales to meet Posthumus, for the sake of bringing into the action Belarius, a banished lord, who has brought up Cymbeline's two long-lost sons. Thus an idyllic element is introduced though the setting is war between Britain and Rome.

It is not my task to go over the complicated and interesting action. There is no difficulty in receiving it as presented by Posthumus. Neither should there be any difficulty in the vision he has in prison. This is supposed to be an interpolation; but I agree with Professor Wilson Knight that it is undoubtedly Shakespeare, and essential to the play. The stage directions for this scene are unusually detailed, and the vision, in which Posthumus's father and two brothers appear, with Jupiter descending in thunder and lightning, is highly impressive. The Jacobean stage had no difficulty with these stage effects, neither should our modern stages with their ample machinery; but usually the vision is cut or omitted altogether as beyond the capacity of present-day theatres and their producers.

All conflicts are reconciled in the last act, as should happen in tragi-comedy:

> Never was a Warr did cease
> (Ere bloodie hands were wash'd) with such a Peace.
>
> (5.5)

The play has an exhilarating effect, and as a whole is highly agreeable.

THE WINTER'S TALE (1611)

This play has not a good stage history, for its strange fairy-tale character could not be accepted, and until Granville Barker made it the first of his famous Shakespeare productions in 1912, when he gave it as written with only six lines cut, it had not held the stage, though there were many different versions following David Garrick's effort to make it credible. As actual life the play is not credible, only as an imaginative presentation of human nature can it give delight, which it does in ample measure.

In this play Shakespeare returns to the intense individuation of his characters. In contrast with Cymbeline, where the characters were somewhat abstractly presented, everything is sharp and clear.

There are two major difficulties. Leontes' unaccountable attack of jealousy, and the hiding of his supposedly dead Queen for sixteen years. If the play is not expected to have the rationality of natural life, these difficulties vanish. For Leontes becomes jealous; how? The answer is simply that he became jealous: the idea flies into his mind; he does not reflect, but acts without thinking; it is impulse: he is a tyrant and behaves as such. These are all familiar motives in Shakespeare, also in life. In the tale from which Shakespeare took the plot Leontes is already jealous. In Shakespeare he is certainly not. Quiller-Couch wanted to think that there was something missing from the play that explains Leontes' jealousy; but Shakespeare had a different aim. He was a dramatist. He let the play open in happiness, which is the important function of the opening scene between the two lords. That was Shakespeare's way, which actors find difficult, so that Leontes usually comes on the stage glowering, but Shakespeare did not intend that he should.

The disappearance of Hermione is intended first to deepen the tragic element, afterwards to heighten the comedy, then to create the opportunity of bringing into the action pastoral loveliness, and finally to make reconciliation complete. From this point of view the play is as near perfection as a drama could be made.

If the play is accepted with Leontes as protagonist, and the action as his vision at the reconciliation, there are no difficulties; it has the sweetness, the sharpness, the pain and the joy of a rare and exalted experience. Nothing Shakespeare wrote has more dramatic delight in it than this play, and nothing more fully illustrates the law of drama.

At the opening the two Kings are renewing their youth. This happiness continues, until suddenly in the second scene, without warning, jealousy of his friend springs fully alive in the mind of Leontes. "Too hot, too hot," he gasps, looking at his Queen, smiling at Polixenes, and he nearly dies with suppressed rage. He can do nothing with himself, and when the two go into the garden takes the audience into his confidence:

> ... there have been
> (Or I am much deceiv'd) Cuckolds ere now,
> And many a man there is (even at this present,
> Now while I speake this) holds his Wife by th's Arme,
> That little thinkes she has been slyc'd in's absence,
> And his Pond fish'd by his next Neighbour, (by
> Sir Smile, his Neighbour:) nay, there's comfort in't,
> Whiles other men have Gates, and those Gates open'd

(As mine) against their will. Should all despaire
That have revolted Wives, the tenth of Mankind
Would hang themselves. Physick for't, theres none :
It is a bawdy Planet, that will strike
Where 'tis predominant: and 'tis powerfull: thinke it:
From East, West, North and South, be it concluded,
No Barricado for a Belly. Know't
It will let in and out the Enemy,
With bag and baggage; many thousand on's
Have the Disease, and feele't not.

(1.2)

A more terrible denunciation of women is not to be found in Shakespeare. Yet there was not the slightest reason for such an outburst from Leontes. Hermione, his Queen, is perfect from the start. There is no flaw in her. As he sees her in vision she is an angel of purity, and so she continues throughout, even when she is tried, when justified by the oracle she is none the less condemned by her vicious spouse, and then seemingly dies.

In rejecting the oracle Leontes defies the gods, and though in sudden remorse he repents, his problem is how to make amends for his folly. He has to suffer for sixteen years. This "wide gap of time" is for the sake of this suffering and to allow the child born before the trial, the child which Leontes has rejected, to grow up and become a lovely girl. She is courted by the enemy-friend King's son, he thinking her to be a shepherd's daughter. No more exquisite scenes appear in the whole of drama than between the two. They have the perfection of vision. This is how Leontes saw them afterwards, in the ecstasy of remorse that lifts the ecstasy of Florizel and Perdita into the realm of divine love. There is not a shadow of natural life upon these exalted, lovely, dream-pictures of pastoral happiness; and though the happiness seems to be disturbed, it is no more than seeming, and leads to eventual joy.

Over all the play there is the sun, the golden sun. At first the hard glare of Sicily that burns in the raging jealousy of Leontes. Yet in the darkness that follows, the excited words are said:

This is Faiery Gold, boy, and 'twill prove so.

(3.3)

Thereafter shines the soft sun of Bohemia, which is nothing but English fairy-land sun; and at the close the sun of reconciled hearts.

The poetry is so delicious, yet much of it so complex and concentrated, that it asks for the perfection of art from the players; and the play's action is so thrilling, yet so touching, that it demands the most faithful devotion to the text from producers. Of all the plays, it is, perhaps, the one in which the participation of the audience is most easily secured and becomes most immediately profitable.

THE TEMPEST (1611)

We know that this play was performed before the King's majesty in the banqueting room at Whitehall on Hallowmas night in 1611, and eighteen months later was again performed at Court before Prince Charles, his sister, Elizabeth, and her suitor the Prince Palatine Elector. It has always been a favourite, though at the Restoration it was adapted and made into an opera. In John Dryden's prologue to the adapted version, for which he was partly responsible, he declared:

But Shakespeare's power is sacred as a king's.

Unfortunately, he did not behave accordingly, neither did Garrick, nor have most producers since. Quiller-Couch said that of all the books written in the world he would choose first The Tempest.

The play is tragi-comedy as are the two that precede it. Its protagonist is Prospero, the exiled Duke of Milan, magician of the island. His problem is the simple one of restoration to his dukedom; but the action is by no means simple, for it is pervaded by magic from start to finish. At the opening there is a storm and shipwreck, which in the next scene we learn to be a work of magic. Thus the play's atmosphere is created; those who attempt to bring it down to earth do so at the peril of their intelligence.

Although magic islands were a pleasant preoccupation of the Jacobean imagination, and shipwrecks made popular stories, this play is Shakespeare's invention. Professor Wilson Knight calls it "an interpretation of Shakespeare's world". It appears to have something of the nature of Shakespeare's own commentary upon his work and everyone has seen Shakespeare in Prospero. And it is true that, while the protagonist in all the plays is Shakespeare speaking, Prospero seems especially near to Shakespeare. Prospero has been betrayed and cast off; was this how Shakespeare saw himself? Prospero's words in the Epilogue are:

> Now I want
> Spirits to enforce: Art to enchant,
> And my ending is despaire,
> Unless I be reliev'd by praier
> Which pierces so, that it assaults
> Mercy itselfe and frees all faults.

Did Shakespeare feel betrayed and rejected? Were his great plays not wanted, either by actors or audience, so that those for whom he worked betrayed him, not understanding what his drama was, and did they turn against his art? This play suggests that a rejected Shakespeare may be the explanation of his leaving the theatre, giving up playwriting, and his death.

There is no need to demonstrate that Prospero is the central figure, or that the entire action of the play is as he presents it, for it is obvious, and no one has disputed it. Prospero lives in a cave, as did Timon. Ariel is a supra-human element, Caliban sub-human, but all the characters appear in a non-realistic light. "We are such stuffe as dreames are made on", is said in the first instance of the characters in the play. They are creatures of imagination, Prospero's imagination, and though there have been real kings of Naples and dukes of Milan, in the play they are dream creations. In a secondary sense, however, the words apply to the natural world, to the theatre itself, the actors, and the audience, for they, too, are the stuff of dreams, and they exist only so long as thought is devoted to them. When the concentration of thought ceases to sustain the solid material world, including our bodies and properties, all fades and leaves not a wrack behind. No play is more rewarding in study, or more inspiring on the stage. It touches the secret of human existence, exhibits the mainspring of human action, and unfolds the mystery of life. There are many points to be noted, the political background, Gonzalo's utopia, and the significance respectively of Ariel and Caliban. The masque is an integral part of the play and ought always to be done in full.

The fact that this note is short does not mean that there is not much to say about the play, but that from the particular point of view from which I am writing its significance is clear.

THE FAMOUS HISTORY OF THE LIFE OF
KING HENRY THE EIGHTH (1613)

The last play is one of the most disputed yet one of the most important of Shakespeare's works. The critics cannot reconcile themselves to its being Shakespeare's. Yet with *The Tempest* in mind, there should be no difficulty. He was careless over the plot, and to some extent over construction, but not over the play's theme or the achievement of his aim. The theme is clear and he does what he sets out to do. Its importance is announced in the Prologue:

> I come no more to make you laugh. Things now
> That beare a Weighty and a Serious Brow,
> Sad, high, and working, full of State and Woe:
> Such noble Scenes, as draw the Eye to flow
> We now present.

He then goes on to comment on the audience, and what is said should be noted:

> Those that can Pitty, heere
> May (if they think it well) let fall a Teare,
> The Subject will deserve it. Such as give
> Their Money out of hope they may believe,
> May heere finde Truth too. Those that come to see
> Only a show or two, and so agree,
> The Play may passe: if they be still and willing
> Ile undertake may see away their shilling
> Richly in two short houres. Onely they
> That come to heare a Merry, Bawdy Play,
> A noyse of Targets: Or to see a Fellow
> In a long Motley Coate, garded with Yellow
> Will be deceiv'd. For gentle Hearers, know
> To ranke our chosen Truth with such a show
> As Foole, and Fight is, beside forfeyting
> Our owne Braines, and the Opinion that we bring
> To make that onely true, we now intend
> Will leave us never an understanding Friend.
> Therefore, for Goodnesse sake, and as you are knowne
> The First and Happiest Hearers of the Towne,
> Be sad, as we would make ye.

By "sad" Shakespeare means "serious", and that the play is "true"
he emphasized; indeed, its early title was *All is True*. It is not
intended to be an entertainment for those who want to be tickled
by the clowns. He goes on, asking for the audience's participation:

> Thinke ye see
> The very Persons of our Noble Story,
> As they were Living: Thinke you see them Great,
> And follow'd with the generall throng, and sweat
> Of thousand Friends: Then, in a moment, see
> How soone this Mightinesse, meets Misery:
> And if you can be merry then, Ile say
> A Man may weepe upon his Wedding day.

I make no apology for quoting this Prologue in full, because it
indicates clearly the playwright's attitude; it is his last play, and all
the more important.

The theme of the play is kingship which is the "chosen Truth".
Its protagonist is the King, and the action is as seen through Henry's
eyes. It is essentially political, the personal issues being only for the
tears of the audience, and altogether it is perhaps Shakespeare's
most important political play. The greatness of kingship, its value to
England, and the greatness of England are what the play is intended
to declare. The King's problem is the future of his country, which is
settled with the birth of Elizabeth.

There are three great people who fall in the play, the Duke of
Buckingham, for treachery against the King; Cardinal Wolsey, for
inordinate ambition conflicting with the function of kingship; and
Queen Katherine, because she did not produce an heir. They evoke
tears; but the fall of none makes the play a tragedy. It is very much
the reverse; for Henry gets his heir, and the foundations of the
Church of England are laid, so that the play ends in rejoicing.

If it be accepted as Henry's vision, as his account of the affairs it
deals with, the play increases in significance. As a mere story it is
touching and impressive, but as an interpretation or meditation upon
national events it sounds depths not elsewhere reached. This means
that the action cannot be carried out by naturalistic playing, but is
required to be dream-like, remote, elevated, and serious. The opening
sets the high level of the action. The Duke and the Cardinal meet,
their enmity is made obvious, and before the scene ends the Duke is
arrested. This is as the King sees it. In the second scene he appears

with the Cardinal, Nobles, and the Queen. The King's concern for the people appears, though he goes sharply against the Cardinal:

> We must not rend our Subjects from our Lawes,
> And sticke them in our Will.
>
> (1.2)

Throughout, the King is set in a good light. The present-day popular idea of King Henry as a heavy, gross, greedy, rude, licentious man should not be read into it. He was, indeed, the reverse, intelligent, graceful, cultivated, violent, dictatorial, and much concerned about the succession, a man to be admired. The play is misinterpreted unless this is observed and the popular idea ignored.

A feature of the play is pageantry. The utmost splendour of staging is required, and in no other play are the stage directions so detailed. Its central feature is the coronation procession of Ann Bullen. Its climax in the speech by Cranmer at the end after the christening of Elizabeth. There is the dream of Queen Katherine just before she dies. It is described in detail, and must be staged, for it is part of Henry's own vision.

In this final play the law of drama has a triumphant justification. Full of faults in the eyes of the critics, the play invariably succeeds on the stage, for it has dramatic effectiveness of the highest order. It is, indeed, a splendid play, fulfilling all that the law of drama demands, and a magnificent conclusion to the work of the dramatist.

CONCLUSION

What I have sought to do all too briefly is to indicate the conception of drama possessed by Shakespeare as exhibited in his plays, to show how that conception developed into maturity as he became master of his art, and to invite attention to the bearing of this informing principle of drama upon the interpretation of his plays. I think what I have attempted, I fear so inadequately, has, perhaps, significance in the understanding of the nature of drama; for if Shakespeare is the supreme dramatist, the principle on which he wrote must mean something to drama wherever it is or has been written. I have thought it possible to formulate what I have called the fundamental law of drama as a matter of interest not only to students of Shakespeare and to all who have to do with the plays, also to all interested in drama, either as spectators, actors, or writers. I have no more than suggested the wider inferences of what I call the "law". To those who object that no law of any kind ought to be admitted in Shakespeare, much less in drama in general, I say that the perception of limits in every human work, whatever its nature, is necessary to its making as well as to its appreciation.

Drama is a particular form or mode of art and in it, as in all art, the presence of structure is explicit, which means limitation, which involves definition. What is inherent in the structure of drama, what is accessory or incidental, and what are irrelevant and impertinent in its making and performance are all valid questions. I have no more than touched upon them, for a much extended study of the nature of drama would have been involved, which is beyond what I have thought possible at this moment. I have confined myself to the examination of Shakespeare's plays and leave the results to others.

As I do not believe Shakespeare to have been an unselfconscious writer, unaware of what he was doing, I do not agree with Granville Barker that the formulation of principles of playwriting is "a mischievous thing". I think there is a fundamental principle, and a simple one, which I have called a "law", and the perception of that law as inherent in Shakespeare is the substance of my contribution.

INDEX

THE PLAYS

THE PROTAGONISTS

NAMES AND SUBJECTS

*Characters in the plays, other than the protagonists, are not indexed
unless referred to on other pages than those concerning the plays in
which they appear.*

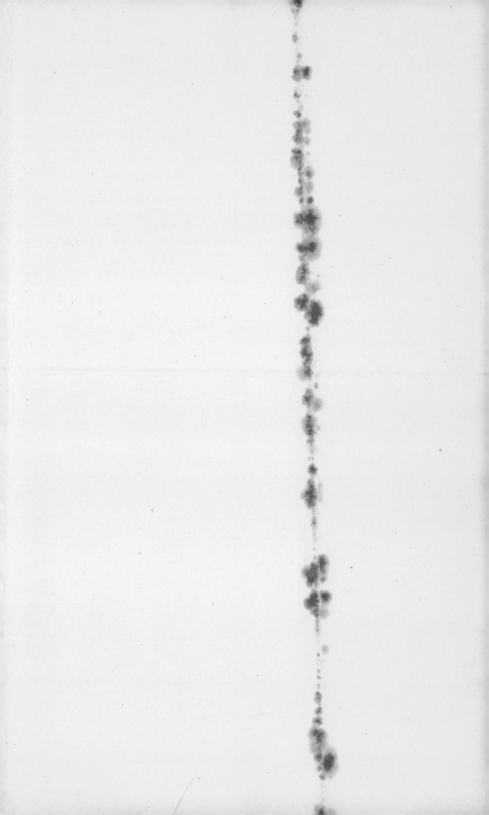